Speeches of the Honorable Jefferson Davis

By

Jefferson Finis Davis

Published by Left of Brain Books

Copyright © 2023 Left of Brain Books

ISBN 978-1-397-66735-9

First Edition

All rights reserved. No part of this publication may be reproduced, distributed, or transmitted in any form or by any means, including photocopying, recording, or other electronic or mechanical methods, without the prior written permission of the publisher, except in the case of brief quotations permitted by copyright law. Left of Brain Books is a division of Left Of Brain Onboarding Pty Ltd.

PUBLISHER'S PREFACE

About the Book

"Jefferson Finis Davis (June 3, 1808 - December 6, 1889) was an American politician who served as President of the Confederate States of America for its entire history from 1861 to 1865 during the American Civil War. During his presidency, Davis was never able to find a strategy that would defeat the larger, more industrially developed Union. Davis's insistence on independence, even in the face of crushing defeat, prolonged the war, and while not exactly disgraced, he was displaced in Southern affection after the war by the leading general, Robert E. Lee. After Davis was captured in 1865, he was charged with treason (although never convicted) and was stripped of his eligibility to run for public office. This limitation was removed in 1978, 89 years after his death. A West Point graduate, Davis prided himself on the military skills he gained in the Mexican-American War as a colonel of a volunteer regiment, and as U.S. Secretary of War under Franklin Pierce."

(Quote from wikipedia.org)

CONTENTS

PUBLISHER'S PREFACE
   TO THE PEOPLE OF MISSISSIPPI 1
   EXTRACTS FROM SPEECHES IN U.S. SENATE 2
   ON FOURTH OF JULY, 1858, AT SEA 5
   SPEECH AT THE PORTLAND SERENADE, JULY 9TH, 1858 9
   SPEECH AT THE PORTLAND CONVENTION 19
   SPEECH AT BELFAST ENCAMPMENT 25
   BANQUET AFTER ENCAMPMENT AT BELFAST 27
   SPEECH AT THE PORTLAND MEETING 35
   SPEECH AT STATE FAIR AT AUGUSTA, ME 49
   SPEECH AT THE GRAND RATIFICATION MEETING, FANEUIL HALL 63
   SPEECH IN THE CITY OF NEW YORK 87
   SPEECH BEFORE THE MISSISSIPPI LEGISLATURE 97

TO THE PEOPLE OF MISSISSIPPI

I have been induced by the persistent misrepresentation of popular Addresses made by me at the North and the South during the year 1858, to collect them, and with extracts from speeches made by me in the Senate in 1850, to present the whole in this connected form; to the end that the case may be fairly before those by whose judgment I am willing to stand or fall.

Jefferson Davis.

EXTRACTS FROM SPEECHES IN U.S. SENATE

IN the Senate of the United States, May 8, 1850, in presenting the Resolutions of the Legislature of Mississippi:

It is my opinion that justice will not be done to the South, unless from other promptings than are about us here--that we shall have no substantial consideration offered to us for the surrender of an equal claim to California. No security against future harassment by Congress will probably be given. The rainbow which some have seen, I fear was set before the termination of the storm. If this be so, those who have been first to hope, to relax their energies, to trust in compromise promises, will often be the first to sound the alarm when danger again approaches. Therefore I say, if a reckless and self-sustaining majority shall trample upon her rights, if the Constitutional equality of the States is to be overthrown by force, private and political rights to be borne down by force of numbers, then, sir, when that victory over Constitutional rights is achieved, the shout of triumph which announces it, before it is half uttered, will be checked by the united, the determined action of the South, and every breeze will bring to the marauding destroyers of those rights, the warning: woe, woe to the riders who trample them down! I submit the report and resolutions, and ask that they may be read and printed for the use of the Senate.--(Cong. Globe, p. 943-4.)

In the Senate of the United States, June 27, 1850, on the Compromise Bill:

If I have a superstition, sir, which governs my mind and holds it captive, it is a superstitious reverence for the Union. If one can inherit a sentiment, I may be said to have inherited this from my revolutionary father. And if education can develop a sentiment in the heart and mind of man, surely mine has been such as would most develop feelings of attachment for the Union. But, sir, I have an allegiance to the State which I represent here. I have an allegiance to those who have entrusted their interests to me, which every consideration of faith and of duty, which every feeling of honor, tells me is above all other political considerations. I trust I shall never find my allegiance there and here in conflict. God forbid that the day should ever come when to be true to my constituents is to be hostile to the Union. If, sir, we have reached that hour in the progress of our institutions, it is past the age to which the Union should have lived. If we have got to the point when it is treason to the United States to protect the rights and interests of our constituents, I ask why should they longer be represented here? why longer remain a part of the Union? If there is a dominant party in this Union which can deny to us equality, and the rights we derive through the Constitution; if we are no longer the freemen our fathers left us; if we are to be crushed by the power of an unrestrained majority, this is not the Union for which the blood of the Revolution was shed; this is not the Union I was taught from my cradle to revere; this is not the Union in the service of which a large portion of my life has been passed; this is not the Union for which our fathers pledged their property, their lives, and sacred honor. No, sir, this would be a central Government, raised on the destruction of all the principles of the Constitution, and the first, the highest obligation of every man who has sworn to support that Constitution would be resistance to such usurpation. This is my position.

My colleague has truly represented the people of Mississippi as ardently attached to the Union. I think he has not gone beyond the truth when he has placed Mississippi one of the first, if not the first, of the States of the Confederation in attachment to it. But, sir, even that deep attachment and habitual reverence for the Union, common to us all--even that, it may become necessary to try by the touchstone of reason. It is not impossible that they should unfurl the flag of disunion. It is not impossible that violations of the Constitution and of their rights, should drive them to that dread extremity. I feel well assured that they will never reach it until it has been twice and three times justified. If, when thus fully warranted, they want a standard bearer, in default of a better, I am at their command.--(Cong. Globe, p. 995-6)

ON FOURTH OF JULY, 1858, AT SEA

[From the Boston Post.]

THE fine ship Joseph Whitney, from Baltimore, Captain S. Howes, was making for this port on the day of the celebration of the nation's birth, and among an unusually brilliant array of passengers from different parts of the country, was the distinguished Senator, Jefferson Davis, of Mississippi. The patriotic suggestion of the captain, to celebrate the day in a manner befitting the great anniversary, met with a hearty response from the company, among whom were zealous republicans, democrats and Americans. A committee was appointed to invite the Senator to make an address, and he consented.

First, the Declaration of Independence was read by Sebastian F. Streeter, Esq., of Baltimore, when Senator Davis made an address of singular felicity of diction and impassioned eloquence, and of such a character as to command the admiration of those who listened to it. He commenced by happy allusions to the array of beauty and intelligence that stood before him from all parts of our common country; he then passed in review the condition of the feeble and separate colonies of 1776, and contrasted with it the country now--the only proper republic on earth, as it stood before the world in its wonderful progress in art, and agriculture, and commerce, and all the elements that constitute a great nation. When thus sailing on the Atlantic, looking to the coast of the United States, he was reminded of those bold refugees from the British and French oppression who crosses these water to found a home in what was then a wilderness. The memory, too, arose of the many sorrowing hearts and oppressed spirits since born over these waves to that refuge from political oppression which our fathers founded as the home of liberty and the asylum of mankind. Her terrtiory {sic}, which now stretches from ocean to ocean, contains a vast interior yet unpeopled; and, with a destiny of still further and continued expansion of area, why should the gate of the temple be now shut upon sorrowing mankind? Rather let it be that the gate should be forever open, and an emblematic flag, hereafter as heretofore, wave a welcome to all to come to the modern Abdella--fugitives from political oppression.

Senator Davis dwelt at some length on the right of search question--on the insulting claim which Great Britain made to a peace-right to visit our ships. Under the pretence of stopping the slave trade--a trade against which the United States was the first nation to raise its voice--she had interrupted and destroyed a lucrative commerce we had enjoyed in ivory and other products on the coast of Africa. The late outrages in the Gulf found us, as a people, with domestic quarrels on our hands; but if this power counted on existing divisions and on making them wider, the result showed how great was her error. The insult was resented by a united people; the Senate, as one man, leaped up against British pretensions; while England, as suddenly, astonished, withdrew her pretensions. The claim she so long preferred is given up--entirely abandoned. The same spirit that resented insult in the past will resent it in the future. I stand, said the Senator, substantially on the deck of an American vessel; it is American soil; the American flag floats over it; its right to course the ocean pathway is perfect. When the blue firmament reflected its own color in the sea, it was the unappropriated property of mankind; and it was arrogant and idle for any nation to deny to the United States her full enjoyment of this common property. It was for the full and undisturbed enjoyment of this right that out fathers, when much less prepared for war than we are now, engaged in the conflict of 1812; and for this right we were ready to strike in 1858. Let a feign power, under any pretence whatever, insult the American flag, and it will find that we are not a divided people, but that a mighty arm will be raised to smite down the insulter, and this great country will continue united.

Trifling politicians in the South, or in the North, or in the West, may continue to talk otherwise, but it will be of no avail. They are like the mosquitoes around the ox: they annoy, but they cannot wound, and never kill. There was a common interest which run through all the diversified occupations and various products of these sovereign States; there was a common sentiment of nationality which beat in every American bosom; there were common memories sweet to us all, and, though clouds had occasionally darkened our political sky, the good sense and the good feeling of the people had thus far averted any catastrophe destructive of our constitution and the Union. It was in fraternity and an elevation of principle which rose superior to sectional or individual aggrandizement that the foundations of our Union were laid; and if we, the present generation, be worthy of our ancestry, we shall not only protect those foundations from destruction, but build higher and wider this temple of liberty, and inscribe perpetuity upon its tablet.

In the course of his beautiful speech, senator Davis passed a noble eulogium on our mother country; and dwelt on the many reasons why the most cordial friendship should be maintained with her; and he concluded by a tribute to the fair sex--the women--beautiful woman; to the wondrous educational influence as the mother which she exercised over the minds of men. It is ever, at all times, felt and operative--upon the dreary waste of ocean, on the lonely prairie, in the troublous contests at the national halls. And when the arm is moved in the deadly conflicts of the battle-field, and the foe is vanquished, then the gentle influences instilled by women do their work, and the heart melts into tears of pity and prompts to deeds of mercy.

After this intellectual repast, then succeeded congratulations; the air was made vocal with song; while, through the foresight of the gallant captain, at the evening hour, the sky about the good ship Joseph Whitney was brilliant with those various pyrotechnic displays which must be so grateful to the spirit of patriotic John Adams, of bonfire and illumination-memory.

SPEECH AT THE PORTLAND SERENADE, JULY 9TH, 1858

AFTER the music had ceased, Mr. Davis appeared upon the steps, and as soon as the prolonged applause with which he was greeted had subsided, he spoke in substance as follows:

Fellow Countrymen:--Accept my sincere thanks for this manifestation of your kindness. Vanity does not lead me so far to misconceive your purpose as to appropriate the demonstration to myself; but it is not less gratifying to me to be made the medium through which Maine tenders an expression of regard to her sister Mississippi. It is moreover, with feelings of profound gratification that I witness this indication of that national sentiment and fraternity which made us, and which alone can keep us, one people. At a period, but as yesterday when compared with the life of nations, these States were separate, and in sorts respects opposing colonies; their only relation to each other was that of a common allegiance to the government of Great Britain. So separate, indeed almost hostile, was their attitude, that when Gen. Stark, of Bennington memory, was captured by savages on the head waters of the Kennebec, he was subsequently taken by them to Albnny {sic} where they went to sell furs, and again led away a captive, without interference on the part of the inhabitants of that neighboring colony to demand or obtain his release. United as we now are, were a citizen of the United States, as an act of hostility to our country, imprisoned or slain in any quarter of the world, whether on land or sea, the people of each and every State of the Union, with one heart, and with one voice, would demand redress, and woe be to him against whom a brother's blood cried to us from the ground. Such is the fruit of the wisdom and the justice with which our fathers bound contending colonies into confederation and blended different habits and rival interests into a harmonious whole, so that shoulder to shoulder they entered on the trial of the revolution, step with step trod its thorny paths until they reached the height of national independence and founded the constitutional representative liberty, which is our birthright.

When the mother country entered upon her career of oppression, in disregard of chartered and constitutional rights, our forefathers did not stop to measure the exact weight of the burden, or to ask whether the pressure bore most upon this colony or upon that, but saw in it the infraction of a great principle, the denial of a common right, in defence of which they made common cause; Massachusetts, Virginia and South Carolina vieing with each other as to who should be foremost in the struggle, where the penalty of failure would be a dishonorable grave.

Tempered by the trials and sacrifices of the revolution, dignified by its noble purposes, elevated by its brilliant triumphs, endeared to each other by its glorious memories, they abandoned the confederacy, not to fly apart when the outward pressure of hostile fleets and armies were removed, but to draw closer their embrace in the formation of a more perfect union. By such men, thus trained and ennobled, our Constitution was formed. It stands a monument of principle, of forecast, and, above all, of that liberality which made each willing to sacrifice local interest, individual prejudice or temporary good to the general welfare, and the perpetuity of the Republican institutions which they had passed through fire and blood to secure. The grants were as broad as were necessary for the functions of the general agent, and the mutual concessions were twice blessed, blessing both him who gave and him who received. Whatever was necessary for domestic government, requisite in the social organization of each community, was retained by the States and the people thereof; and these it was made the duty of all to defend and maintain.

Such, in very general terms, is the rich political legacy our fathers bequeathed to us. Shall we preserve and transmit it to posterity? Yes, yes, the heart responds, and the judgment answers, the task is easily performed. It but requires that each should attend to that which most concerns him, and on which alone he has rightful power to decide and to act. That each should adhere to the terms of a written compact and that all should cooperate for that which interest, duty and honor demand. For the general affairs of our country, both foreign and domestic, we have a national executive and a national legislature. Representatives and Senators are chosen by districts and by States, but their acts affect the whole country, and their obligations are to the whole people. He who holding either seat would confine his investigations to the mere interests of his immediate constituents would be derelict to his plain duty; and he who would legislate in hostility to any section would be morally unfit for the station, and surely an unsafe depositary if not a treacherous guardian of the inheritance with which we are blessed.

No one, more than myself; recognizes the binding force of the allegiance which the citizen owes to the State of his citizenship, but that State being a party to our compact, a member of our union, fealty to the federal Constitution is not in opposition to, but flows from the allegiance due to one of the United States. Washington was not less a Virginian when he commanded at Boston; nor did Gates or Greene weaken the bonds which bound them to their several States, by their campaigns in the

South. In proportion as a citizen loves his own State, will he strive to honor by preserving her name and her fame free from the tarnish of having failed to observe her obligations, and to fulfil her duties to her sister States. Each page of our history is illustrated by the names and the deeds of those who have well understood, and discharged the obligation. Have we so degenerated, that we can no longer emulate their virtues? Have the purposes for which our Union was formed, lost their value? Has patriotism ceased to be a virtue, and is narrow sectionalism no longer to be counted a crime? Shall the North not rejoice that the progress of agriculture in the South has given to her great staple the controlling influence of the commerce of the world, and put manufacturing nations under bond to keep the peace with the United States? Shall the South not exult in the fact, that the industry and persevering intelligence of the North, has placed her mechanical skill in the front ranks of the civilized world--that our mother country, whose haughty minister some eighty odd years ago declared that not a hob-nail should be made in the colonies, which are now the United States, was brought some four years ago to recognize our pre-eminence by sending a commission to examine our work shops, and our machinery, to perfect their own manufacture of the arms requisite for their defence? Do not our whole people, interior and seaboard, North, South, East, and West, alike feel proud of the hardihood, the enterprise, the skill, and the courage of the Yankee sailor, who has borne our flag far as the ocean bears its foam, and caused the name and the character of the United States to be known and respected wherever there is wealth enough to woo commerce, and intelligence enough to honor merit? So long as we preserve, and appreciate the achievements of Jefferson and Adams, of Franklin and Madison, of Hamilton, of Hancock, and of Rutledge, men who labored for the whole country, and lived for mankind, we cannot sink to the petty strife which would sap the foundations, and destroy the political fabric our fathers erected, and bequeathed as an inheritance to our posterity forever.

Since the formation of the Constitution, a vast extension of territory, and the varied relations arising there from, have presented problems which could not have been foreseen. It is just cause for admiration--even wonder, that the provisions of the fundamental law should have been found so fully adequate to all the wants of government, new in its organization, and new in many of the principles on which it was founded. Whatever fears may have once existed as to the consequences of territorial expansion, must give way before the evidence which the past affords. The general government, strictly confined to its delegated functions, and the States left in the undisturbed exercise of all else, we have a theory and practice which fits our government for immeasurable domain, and might, under a millennium of nations, embrace mankind.

From the slope of the Atlantic our population with ceaseless tide has poured into the wide and fertile valley of the Mississippi, with eddying whirl has passed to the coast of the Pacific, from the West and the East the tides are rushing towards each other--and the mind is carried to the day when all the cultivable and will be inhabited, and the American people will sign for more wildernesses to conquer. But there is here a physico-political problem presented for our solution. Were it was purely physical--your past triumphs would leave but little doubt of your capacity to solve it.

A community, which, when less than twenty thousand, conceived the grand project of crossing the White Mountains, and, unaided, save by the stimulus which jeers and prophecies of failure gave, successfully executed the herculean work, might well be impatient, if it were suggested that a physical problem was before us, too difficult for their mastery. The history of man teaches that high mountains and wide deserts have resisted the permanent extension of empire, and have formed the immutable boundaries of States. From time to time, under some able leader, have the hordes of the upper plains of Asia swept over the adjacent country, and rolled their conquering columns over Southern Europe. Yet, after the lapse of a few generations, the physical law to which I have referred, has asserted its supremacy, and the boundaries of those States differ little now from those which obtained three thousand years ago. Rome flew her conquering eagles over the then known world, and has now subsided into the little territory on which her great city was originally built. The Alps and the Pyrenees have been unable to restrain imperial France; but her expansion was a leverish action; her advance and her retreat were tracked with blood, and those mountain ridges are the re-established limits of her empire. Shall the Rocky Mountains prove a dividing barrier to us? Were ours a central consolidated government, instead of a Union of sovereign States, our fate might be learned from the history of other nations. Thanks to the wisdom and independent spirit of our forefathers, this is not our case. Each State having sole charge of its local interests and domestic affairs, the problem which to others has been insoluble, to us is made easy. Rapid, safe, and easy communication and co-operation among all parts of our continent-wide republic. The network of railroads which bind the North and the South, the slope of the Atlantic and the valley of the Mississippi, together testify that our people have the power to perform, in that regard, whatever it is their will to do.

We require a railroad to the States of the Pacific for present uses; the time no doubt will come when we shall have need of two or three; it may be more. Because of the desert character of the interior country the work will be difficult and expensive. It will require the efforts of an united people. The bickerings of little politicians, the jealousies of sections, must give way to dignity of purpose and zeal for the common good. If the object be obstructed by contention and division as to whether the route to be selected shall be northern, southern or central, the handwriting is on the wall, and it requires little skill to see that failure is the interpretation of the inscription. You are a practical people and may ask, how is that contest to be avoided? By taking the question out of the hands of politicians altogether. Let the Government give such aid as it is proper for it to render to the Company which shall propose the most feasible and advantageous plan; then leave to capitalists with judgment sharpened by interest, the selection of the route, and the difficulties will diminish as did those which you overcame when you connected your harbor with the Canadian Provinces.

It would be to trespass on your kindness and to violate the proprieties of the occasion, were I to detain the vast concourse which stands before me, by entering on the discussion of controverted topics, or by further indulging in the expression of such reflections as circumstances suggest.

I came to your city in quest of health and repose. From the moment I entered it you have showered upon me kindness and hospitality. Though my experience has taught me to anticipate good rather than evil from my fellow man, it had not prepared me to expect such unremitting attention as has here been bestowed. I have been jocularly asked in relation to my coming here, whether I had secured a guaranty {sic} for my safety, and lo, I have found it. I stand in the midst of thousands of my fellow citizens. But my friend, I came neither distrusting, not apprehensive, of which you have proof in the fact that I brought with me the objects of tenderest affection and solicitude--my wife and my children; they have shared with me your hospitality, and will alike remain your debtors. If at some future time, when I am mingled with the dust, and the arm of my infant son has been nerved for deeds of manhood, the storm of war should burst upon your city, I feel that, relying upon his inheriting the instincts of his ancestors and mine, I may pledge him in that perilous hour to stand by your side in the defence of your hearth stones, and in maintaining the honor of a flag whose constellation though torn and smoked in many a battle, by sea and land, has never been stained with dishonor, and will I trust forever fly as free as the breeze which unfolds it.

A stranger to you, the salubrity of your location and the beauty of its scenery were not wholly unknown to me, nor were there wanting associations which bust memory connected with your people. You will pardon me for alluding to one whose genius shed a lustre upon all it touched, and whose qualities gathered about him hosts of friends, wherever he was known. Prentiss, a native of Portland, lived from youth to middle age in the county of my residence, and the inquiries which have been made, show me that the youth excited the interest which the greatness of the man justified, and that his memory thus remains a link to connect your home with mine.

A cursory view, when passing through your town on former occasions, had impressed me with the great advantages of your harbor, its easy entrance, its depth, and its extensive accommodation for shipping. But its advantages, and if facilities as they have been developed by closer inspection, have grown upon me until I realize that it is no boast, but the language of sober truth which in the present state of commerce pronounces them unequaled in any harbor of our country.

And surely no place could be more inviting to an invalid who sought a refuge from the heat of a southern summer. Here waving elms offer him shared walks, and magnificent residences surrounded by flowers, fill the mind with ideas of comfort and of rest. If weary of constant contact with his fellow men, he seeks a deeper seclusion, there, in the back ground of this grand amphitheatre, lie the eternal mountains, frowning with brow of rock and cap of snow upon the smiling fields beneath, and there in its recesses may be found as much of wildness, and as much of solitude, as the pilgrim weary of the cares of life can desire. If he turn to the front, your capacious harbor, studded with green islands of ever varying light and shade, and enlivened by all the stirring evidences of commercial activity, offer him the mingled charms of busy life and nature's calm repose. A few miles further, and he may site upon the quiet shore to listen to the murmuring wave until the troubled spirit sinks to rest, and in the little sail that vanishes on the illimitable sea, we may find the type of the voyage which he is so soon to take, when, his ephemeral existence closed, he embarks for that better state which lies beyond the grave.

Richly endowed as you are by nature in all which contributes to pleasure and to usefulness, the stranger cannot pass without paying a tribute to the much which your energy has achieved for yourselves. Where else will one find a more happy union of magnificence and comfort, where better arrangements to facilitate commerce? Where so much of industry, with so little noise and bustle? Where, in a phrase, so much effected in proportion to the means employed? We hear the puff of the engine, the roll of the wheel, the ring of the axe, and the saw, but the stormy, passionate exclamations so often mingled with the sounds, are no where heard. Yet, neither these nor other things which I have mentioned; attractive though they be, have been to me the chief charm which I have found among you. For above all these I place the gentle kindness, the cordial welcome, the hearty grasp, which made me feel truly and at once, though wandering far, that I was still at home.

My friends, I thank you for this additional manifestation of your good will.

SPEECH AT THE PORTLAND CONVENTION

ON Thursday, August 24th, 1858, when the Democratic Convention had nearly concluded its business, a committee was appointed to wait on Mr. Davis, and request him to gratify them by his presence in the Convention. He expressed his willingness to comply with the wishes of his countrymen, and accordingly repaired to the City Hall. On entering he was greeted in the most cordial and enthusiastic manner. After business was finished, he proceeded to the rostrum, and, addressing the Convention, said:

Friends, fellow-citizens, and brethren in Democracy, he thanked them for the honor conferred by their invitation to be present at their deliberations, and expressed the pleasure he felt in standing in the midst of the Democracy of Maine--amidst so many manifestations of the important and gratifying fact that the Democratic is, in truth, a national party. He did not fail to remember that the principles of the party declaring for the largest amount of personal liberty consistent with good government, and to the greatest possible extent of community and municipal independence, would render it in their view, as in his own, improper for him to speak of those subjects which were local in their character, and he would endeavor not so far to trespass upon their kindness as to refer to anything which bore such connection, direct or indirect--and he hoped that those of their opponents who, having the control of type, fancied themselves licensed to manufacture facts, would not hold them responsible for what he did not say. He said he should carry with him, as one of the pleasant memories of his brief sojourn in Maine, the additional assurance, which intercourse with the people had given him, that there still lives a National Party, struggling and resolved bravely to struggle for the maintenance of the Constitution, the abatement of sectional hostility, and the preservation of the fraternal compact made by the Fathers of the Republic. He said, rocked in the cradle of Democracy, having learned its precepts from his father,--who was a Revolutionary Soldier--and in later years having been led forward in the same doctrine by the patriot statesman--of whom such honorable mention was made in their resolutions--Andrew Jackson, he had always felt that he had in his own heart a standard by which to measure the sentiments of a Democrat. When, therefore, he had seen evidences of a narrow sectionalism, which sought not the good of the whole, not even the benefit of a part, but aimed at the injury of a particular section, the pulsations of his own heart told him such cannot be the purpose, the aim, or the wish of any American Democrat--and he saw around him to-day evidence that his opinion in this respect had here its verification. As he looked upon the weather-beaten faces of the veterans and upon the flushed cheek and flashing eye of the youth, which told of the fixed resolve of the one, and the ardent, noble hopes of the other, strengthened hope and bright anticipations filled his mind, and he feared not to ask the questions shall narrow interests, shall local jealousies, shall disregard of the high purposes for which our Union was ordained, continue to distract our people and impede the progress of our government toward the high consummation which prophetic statesmen have so often indicated as her destiny?--[Voices, no, no, no! Much applause.]

Thanks for that answer; let every American heart respond no; let every American head, let every American hand unite in the great object of National development. Let our progress be across the land and over the sea, let our flag as stated in your resolutions, continue to wave its welcome to the oppressed, who flee from the despotism of other lands, until the constellation which marks the number of our States which have already increased from thirteen to thirty two, shall go on multiplying into a bright galaxy covering the field on which we now display the revered stripes, which record the original size of our political family, and shall shed its benign light over all mankind, to point them to the paths of self-government and constitutional liberty.

He here referred to the history of the Democratic party, and numbered among its glories the various acts of territorial acquisition and triumphs through its foreign intercourse in the march of civilization and National amity, as well as in the glories which from time to time had been shed by the success of our arms upon the name and character of the American people. He alluded to the recent attempt by some of the governments of Europe, to engraft upon National law a prohibition against privateering. He said whenever other governments were willing to declare that private property should be exempt from the rigors of war, on sea as it is on land, our government might meet them more than half way, but to a proposition which would leave private property the prey of national vessels and thus give the whole privateering to those governments which maintained a large naval establishment in time of peace, he would unhesitatingly answer no. Our merchant marine constituted the militia of the sea--how effective it had been in our last struggle with a maritime power, he need not say to the sons of those who had figured so conspicuously in that species of warfare. The policy of our government was peace. We could not consent to bear the useless expense of a naval establishment larger than was necessary for its proper uses in a time of peace. Relying as we had and must hereafter upon the merchant marine to man whatever additional vessels we should require, and upon the bold and hardy Yankee sailor, when he could no longer get freight for his craft, to receive a proper armament, and go forth like a knight errant of the sea in quest of adventure against the enemies of his country's flag.

He said our country was powerful for all military purposes, and if asked to compare her armies and her navy with those of the great powers of Europe, he would answer, that is not our standard. History teaches that our strength is in the courage and patriotism, the skill and intelligence of our people. A part of the American army was before him, and a part of the American navy was lying in the harbor of their city. That army and that navy had fought the battles of the Revolution, of the "war of 1812" and of the war with Mexico, and would never be found wanting, whilst the patriotism of the earlier days of the Republic, proved a sufficient cement to hold the different parts of our wide spread and extending country together. He said that everything around him spoke eloquently of the wisdom of the men who founded these colonies-their descendants, who sat before him, contrasted strongly, as did their history and present power, stand out in bold relief, when compared with those of the inhabitants of Central and Southern America. Chief among the reasons for this, he believed to be the self-reliant hardihood of their forefathers who, when but a handful, found themselves confronted by hordes of savages, yet proudly maintained the integrity of their race and asserted its supremacy over the descendants of Shem, in whose tents they had come to dwell. They preferred to encounter toil, privation and carnage, rather than debase their lineage and race. Their descendants of that pure and heroic blood have advanced to the high standard of civilization attainable by that type of mankind. Stability and progress, wealth and comfort, art and science, have followed their footsteps.

Among our neighbors of Central and Southern America, we see the Caucasian mingled with the Indian and the African. They have the forms of free government, because they have copied them. To its benefits they have not attained, because that standard of civilization is above their race. Revolution succeeds Revolution, and the country mourns that some petty chief may triumph, and through a sixty days' government ape the rulers of the earth. Even now the nearest and strongest of these American Republics, which were fashioned after the model of our own, seems to be tottering to a fall, and the world is inquiring as to who will take possession; or, as protector, raise and lead a people who have shown themselves incompetent to govern themselves.

He said our fathers laid the foundation of Empire, and declared its purposes; to their sons it remained to complete their superstructure. The means by which this end was to be secured were simple and easy. It involved no harder task than that each man should attend to his own business, that no community should arrogantly assume to interfere with the affairs of another--and that all by the honorable obligation of fulfiling that compact which their fathers had made.

He then referred to the commercial position of Maine, and spoke of her brightly unfolding prospects of prosperity and greatness. Many considered her wealth to consist of her forests, and that her prosperity would decline when her timber was exhausted--he held to a different opinion, and thought they might welcome the day, when the sombre shadows of the Pine gave place to verdant pastures and fruitful fields. Was he asked, what then was to become of the interest of ship-building? He would answer--let it be changed from wood to iron. The skill to be aquired be a few years' experience, would at a fair price for iron, enable our ship builders to construct iron ships, which, taking into account their greater capacity for freight and greater durability, would be cheaper than vessels of wood, even whilst timber was as abundant as now;--at least such was the information he had derived from persons well informed upon those subjects.

He expressed the gratification he felt for the courtesy of the Democracy in Maine, and doubted not that the Democracy of Mississippi would receive it, with grateful recognition, as evincing fraternal sentiment by kindness done to one of her sons, not the less a representative, because a humble member of her Democracy.

SPEECH AT BELFAST ENCAMPMENT

ABOUT the o'clock the troops at the encampment being under arms, Col. Davis was escorted to the ground and reviewed them. He was then introduced to the troops by Gen. Cushman, as follows--

Officers and fellow soldiers, I introduce to you Col. Jefferson Davis, an eminent citizen of Mississippi,--a man, and I say a hero, who has, in the service of his country, been among and faced hostile guns.

Col. Davis replied as follows--

Citizen Soldiers:--I feel pleased and gratified at the exhibition I have witnessed of the military spirit and instruction of the volunteer militia of Maine. I acknowledge the compliment which has been paid to me, and I welcome it as the indication of the liberality and national sentiment which makes the militia of each State the effective, as they are the constitutional defenders of our whole country.

To one who loves his country in all its parts, it is natural to rejoice in whatever contributes to the prosperity and honor, and marks the stability and progress of any portion of its people. I therefore look upon the evidence presented to me of the soldierly enthusiasm and military acquirements displayed on this occasion, with none the less pleasure because I am the citizen of another and distant State. It was not the policy of our government to maintain large armies of navies in time of peace. The history of our past wars established the fact that it was not needful to do so. The militia had bee found equal to all the emergencies of war. Their patriotism, their intelligence, their knowledge of the use of arms, had given to then all the efficiency of veterans, and on many bloody fields they have shown their superiority over the disciplined troops of their enemies. A people morally and intellectually equal to self-government, must also be equal in self-defence. My friends, your worthy General has alluded to my connection with the military service of the country. The memory arose to myself when the troops this day marched past me, and when I looked upon their manly bearing and firm step. I thought could I have seen them thus approaching the last field of battle on which I served, where the changing tide several times threatened disaster to the American flag, with what joy I would have welcomed those striped and starred banners, the emblem and the guide of the free and the brave, and with what pride would the heart have beaten when welcoming the danger's hour, brethren from so remote an extremity of our expanded territory.

One of the evidences of the fraternal confidence and mutual reliance of our fathers was to be found in their compact or mutual protection and common defence. So long as their sons preserve the spirit and appreciate the purpose of their fathers, the United States will remain invincible, their power will grow with the lapse of time, and their example show brighter and brighter as revolving ages roll over the temple our fathers dedicated to constitutional liberty, and founded upon truths announced to their sons, but intended for mankind. I thank you, citizen soldiers, for this act of courtesy. It will long and gratefully be remembered, as a token of respect to the distant State of which I am a citizen, and I trust will be noted by others, as indicating that national sentiment which made, and which alone can preserve us a nation.

BANQUET AFTER ENCAMPMENT AT BELFAST

THE Mayor then gave:

The heroes who have fought our country's battles: may their services be appreciated by a grateful people.

Loud calls being made for Col. Jefferson Davis, that gentleman arose and said:

The sentiment to which he was called to respond excited memories which called up proud emotions, though their associations were sad. He could not reply to a compliment paid to the gallantry of his comrades in the war with Mexico, without remembering how many of them now mingle with the dust of a foreign land, and how many of them have sunk after the day of toil was done by reason of the exposure endured in the service of their country. The land has mourned, and still mourns, the fall of its bravest and best, and truly are our laurels mingled with the cypress, 'tis well, and 'tis wise, 'tis natural and 'tis proper, that in looking on the laurels of our glory we should pause to pay a tribute to the cypress which weeps over them, and having paid this tribute to the gallant dead, the memory of whose service can never die, we pass to the consideration of their acts, and the beneficial results which their sacrifices have secured. When that war begun, our history recorded evidence only of the power of our people for defence. The Fabian policy of Washington, admirably adapted to the condition of the Colonies, achieved so much in proportion to the means, that he would be rash indeed who should attempt to criticise it. The prudent, though daring course of Jackson, fruitful as it was of the end to be attained, did not yet serve to illustrate the capacity of our people for the trials and the struggles attendant on the operations of an invasive war. Hence it was commonly asserted that the American people, though they might resist attack, were powerless to redress aggression which was not connected with the invasion of their territory. The idea of reliance upon undisciplined militia was treated with contempt and derision. To borrow a simile from the pit, we were regarded as dung-hill soldiers, who would only fight at home. In the war with Mexico our armies carried their banners over routes hitherto unknown, through mountain passes where nature had almost completed the work of defence, and penetrated further into the enemy's country than any European army has ever marched from the source of its supplies. Not to prolong the comparison by a reference to events of a remote period, he would only refer to the last campaign in European war. The combined armies of France and England, after preparation worthy of their great military power, advanced through friendly territory to the outer verge of the country, against which they directed a war of invasion, and after a prolonged siege by sea and by land, finally captured a seaport town which they could not hold. Before them lay the country they had come to invade, but there, at the outer gate, their march was arrested, and in sight of the ships which brought them supplies and reinforcements, they terminated a campaign, the scale and proclaimed objects of which had caused the world to look on in expectation of achievements the like of which man had not seen. Why was it so? was it not that they were unable to move from the depot of supplies, though a distance less than half of that over which our army passed before reaching a productive region would have brought the allied forces to a country filled with all the supplies necessary for the support of an army. Is it boastful to say that American troops, and an American treasury, would have encountered and have overcome such an obstacle? He did not forget the complaints which had been made on account of the vast expenditures which had been made in the prosecution of the war with Mexico; but he remembered with pride the capacity which the country had exhibited to bear such expenditure, and believed that our people had no money standard by which to measure the duty of their government, and the honor of their flag. We bear with us from the wars in which we have been engaged no other memory of their cost than the loss of the gallant dead. To the printed reports and tabular statements we must go when we desire to know how many dollars were expended. The successful soldier when he returns from the field is met by a welcome proportionate to the leaves which he has added to the wreath of his country's glory. Each has his reward; to one, the admiring listener at the hearthstone; to another, the triumphal reception; to all, the respect which patriotism renders to patriotic service. To the soldier who, in the early part of the Mexican war, set the seal of invincibility upon American arms, and subsequently by a signal victory dispersed and disorganized the regular army of Mexico, his countrymen voted the highest reward known to our government. Twice before have the people in like manner manifested their approbation and esteem. Thus has the military spirit of the country been nursed; to-day it needs not the monarchial bundles of ribbons, orders and titles to sustain it. Thus has the American citizen been made to realize that it is sweet and honorable to die for one's country; and to feel proudest among his family memories of the names of those who successfully fought or bravely died in defence of the national flag. Often he had had occasion to feel, and to mark the mingled sensation of pride and of sorrow with which friends revert to those who gallantly died in the field. Even at this now remote day he could not travel in Mississippi without having the recollection of his fallen comrades painfully revived by meeting a mother who mourns her son with the agony of a mother's grief; a father, whose stern nature vainly struggles to conceal the involuntary pang, or tender children who know not the extent of their deprivation, though it is indeed the sorest of all. Let none then be surprised that he could not see thee laurel save through the solemn shade of the cypress. Time, however, softened the shadow long before it withers the leaf. On his way to this place he learned that it was possible, and he seized the occasion to visit the residence of Gen. Knox, of revolutionary memory. His own desire to see something which had been identified with a patriot soldier who had so largely contributed to the success of the revolution, and the establishment of the institutions we inherited, was but an indication of the military sentiment which lives in the American heart. It turns the step of the traveller from his direct path, it attracts the boy in his first reading, it fires the ambition of the youth, and encircles the veteran with the kindness of his neighbors, and swells the train which follows his bier when, his duty to his country performed, he answers the summons of his God, and is translated to a better sphere. It is that same military enthusiasm which calls you from the avocations and the pleasures of home to the duties and discomforts of the camp, that you may prepare yourselves whenever your country needs it to render her efficient service. On the militia of the country the rights of its citizens, and the honor of its flag, must mainly depend in the event of a war; they only need to be organized and instructed to render them a secure reliance. Mingled with the great body of the people, identified with their feelings and their interests, proud of the prowess of their fathers and jealousy careful of the country's honor, if properly instructed and prepared, the first trumpet call should bring from plain and from mountain a citizen soldiery who would encircle the land and check the invader with a wall of fire. Your plan of encampment seems best suited to the purposes of practical instruction. A pilgrim in search of health, his steps had been fortunately directed to Maine, the courtesy of the commander of this encampment had induced him to visit it and to review the troops. In all respects it had been to him most gratifying. The appointments, the movements, the stern faces, and stalwart forms of the men, spoke of the power to do, and the will to dare whatever it was needful and proper to perform. This day to manifest respect to a citizen of a distant State, whose only claim upon them is that he has been an American soldier, and is an American citizen, they had cheerfully marched through heavy mire. So much had they given to so small a demand on their natural sentiment, he could not doubt they would with equal alacrity, and with the same firm step, march over a field miry with the blood of comrade and of foe, where opposing causes make to men a common fate.

Among the objects which were of interest to him and which he had hoped to visit, was the fortification at the narrows of the Penobscot. During the last session of congress he had endeavored to obtain an appropriation for the completion of the work which had advanced to the point which made it effective against shipping, but left still liable to be carried by land attack. He was not of those who thought it necessary to raise walls wherever an enemy might land and march, for he would say that henceforward there would remain to an invading army but to choose between captivity and a grave. To protect commercial ports against naval assault forts are needful and should be completed so as to render them defensible by small garrisons, and to save those garrisons as far as possible from the sacrifice of life. Our people require no wall to separate them from other countries, unless it be needful for our own restraint. Our policy is peace, and the fact shines brightly on the pages of our history that not one acre of its extensive acquisitions have been claimed as the spoil of the sword. Unpeopled deserts have been purchased, and on its own application a community has been admitted to our family of states. But we have offered to the world the singular example of conquered territory returned to the vanquished.

Permit me in this connection, whilst ever mindful of the just relation and necessity for concurrent action between the civil and military departments of government, to bear testimony to the value of the militia for the purposes of peace. The principle of self-government and the spirit of independence are so deep rooted in the American mind that our people would illy brook the enforcement of law by any extraneous power, and it is to be hoped we never will see a case in which the people of a State will not be able to maintain the civil authority, and vindicate offended law against all opposers whomsoever. To give energy and activity to such popular action the organization of the militia will be most convenient whenever force shall be needful. It is not a little remarkable that though the first Presidents in emphatic language from time to time recommended a thorough organization of the militia as one of the most important duties of the government, but little more has yet been done than to make provisions for supplying them with arms, and for calling them out when required for federal purposes. There is a moral effect arising from the spectacle of each State possessed of a body of instructed militia, ready not only to maintain its government at home, but to unite with the militia of other States and to form an army upon which all can rely whenever a common danger calls for a common defence. It has been thus that from time to time the fraternity of our revolutionary fathers has been renewed among their sons, and additional assurance has been given that the sentiment of nationality on which our Union was founded could never die. That the expansion of the circle did not weaken its cohesive power, nor the piling of arch upon arch endanger the foundation on which our political temple was built. It was not a structure of expediency; master workmen cleared away the surface where the errors and prejudices of ages had accumulated, dug deep down to the unmutable rock of truth, and with unchanging principles constructed the walls to stand till time should become eternity. Who is there, then, forgetful of his revolutionary descent, insensible to the pride which the name of the United States justly inspires, faithless to the duty which the bond of his fathers imposes, and reckless of all which the honorable discharge of that duty ensures, would unite with impious purpose to destroy that foundation, and strive, with sacrilegious hand to tear the flag under which we had marched from colonial dependence to our present national greatness. Away with speculative theories, and false philanthropy of abstractions, which tend to destroy one half, one third, aye, or a single star of that bright constellation which lights the pathway of our future career, and sends a hopeful ray through the clouds of despotism which hang over less favored lands.

Our mission is not that of propagandists--our principles forbid interference with the institutions of other countries; but we may hope that our example will be imitated, and should so live that this model of representative liberty, community independence, and government derived from the consent of the governed, and limited by a written compact, should commend itself to the adoption of others. We now stand isolated among the great nations of the earth; the opposition of monarchial governments to the theory on which ours is founded, points to the possibility of an alliance against us, by which what is termed national law may be modified and warped to our prejudice if not to our assailment. It needs the united power, harmonious action and concentrated will of the people of all these States to roll the wheel of progress to the end which our fathers contemplated, and which their sons, if they are wise and true, may behold. May the kindness and courtesy which have characterized the present occasion on which Mississippi has been greeted by Maine, be a type of the feeling which shall ever exist between the extremes of our common country. From Florida to California, from Oregon to Maine, from the centre to the remotest border, may the possessors of our constitutional heritage appreciate its value, and faithfully, fraternally labor for its thorough development, looking back to the original compact for the purposes for which the Union was established, and forward to the blessing which such union was designed and is competent to confer.

SPEECH AT THE PORTLAND MEETING

WHEN it became known that Mr. Davis had arrived at the Hall, he was loudly called for. Hon. Joseph Howard, chairman of the meeting, then introduced Mr. Davis, who, on coming forward, was greeted with cheer upon cheer from the vast audience. As soon as the prolonged and enthusiastic applause with which he was welcomed had subsided, Mr. Davis, addressing the audience as fellow citizens and Democratic brethren, said that the invitation with which he had been favored to address them, evinced a purpose to confer together for the common good--for the maintenance of the constitution, the bond of union. He would not be expected to discuss local questions; he would not in this imitate the mischievous agitators who inflame the Northern mind against the Southern States. He came among them, an invalid, advised by his physician to resort to this clime for the restoration of his health; as an American citizen, he had not expected that his right to come here would be questioned; as a stranger, or if not entirely so, known mainly by the detraction which the ardent advocacy of the rights of the South had brought upon him, he had supposed that neither his coming nor his going would attract attention. But his anticipations had proved erroneous. The polite, the manly, elevated men, lifted above the barbarism which makes stranger and enemy convertible terms, had chosen, without political distinction, to welcome his coming, and by constant acts of generous hospitality to make his sojourn as pleasant as his physical condition would permit.

On the other hand, men who make a trade of politics, and whose capital consists in the denunciation of the institutions of other States, had erroneously judged him by themselves, and had regarded his coming as a political mission; wherefore it was, he was led to suppose, that the scavengers of that party had been employed in the publication of falsehoods, both in relation to himself and his political friends at the South.

So far as it affected him personally their attacks were no more than the barking of a cur, which, by its clamor, indicates the inhospitable character of the master who keeps him. If his friends and himself were, as had been falsely charged, Disunionists and Nullifiers, they might naturally have looked for kinder considerations from a party which circulates petitions for a "prompt and peaceful dissolution of the Union" on account of the incompatibility of the sections--from a party, which, having proved faithless to the obligation of the constitution in relation to the fugitive from service or labor, then declares null and void the law which their dereliction made it necessary for Congress to enact. The fealty of himself and friends to the constitution, and their honorable discharge of its obligations was their rebuke to this party, in whose hostility he found the highest commendation in their power to bestow.

By reckless fabrication, by garbling and inserting new words into extracts, they had attempted to deceive the people here as to his opinions, and had crowned the fraud by the absurd announcement that his was the creed on which the people of Maine must vote next Monday.

It was due to the hospitality which he had received at their hands that he should not interfere in their domestic affairs, and he had not failed to remember the obligation; when republicans had introduced the subject of African slavery he had defended it, and answered pharisaical pretensions by citing the Bible, the constitution of the United States and the good of society in justification of the institutions of the State of which he was a citizen; in this he but exercised the right of a freeman and discharged the duty of a Southern citizen. Was it for this cause that he had been signalized as a slavery propagandists? He admitted in all its length and breadth the right of the people of Maine to decide the question for themselves; he held that it would be an indecent interference, on the part of a citizen of another State, if he should arraign the propriety of the judgment they had rendered, and that there was no rightful power in the federal government or in all the States combined, to set aside the decision which the community had made in relation to their domestic institutions. Should any attempt be made thus to disturb their sovereign right, he would pledge himself in advance, as a State-rights man, with his head, his heart and his hand, if need be, to aid them in the defence of this right of community independence, which the Union was formed to protect, and which it was the duty of every American citizen to preserve and to guard as the peculiar and prominent feature of our government.

Why, then, this accusation? Do they fear to allow Southern men to converse with their philosophers, and seek thus to silence or exclude them? He trusted others would contemn them as he did, and that many of our brethren of the South would, like himself, learn by sojourn here, to appreciate the true men of Maine, and to know how little are the political abolitionists and the abolition papers the exponents of the character and the purposes of the Democracy of this State.

And now having brushed away the cob-webs which lay in his path, he would proceed to the consideration of subjects worthy of the audience he had the honor to address.

Democrats, patriots, by whatever political name any of you may be known, you have a sacred duty to perform to your ancestry and to posterity. The time is at hand when for good or for evil, the questions which have agitated the public mind are to be solved. Is it true as asserted by northern agitators that there is such contrariety between the North and the South that they cannot remain united! Or rather, is it not true as our fathers deemed it, that diversity in the character of the population, in the products and in the institutions of the several States formed a reason for their union and tended to secure to their posterity the liberty which was the common object of their love, and by cultivating untrammeled intercourse and free trade between the States, to duplicate the comforts of all?

There was a time when the test of patriotism was the readiness to sever the bond which bound the colonies to the mother country. Recently our people with joyous acclamation have welcomed the connection of the United States with Great Britain, by the Atlantic cable. The one is not inconsistent with the other. When the home government violated the charters of the colonies, and assumed to control the private interests of individuals, the love of political liberty, the determination at whatever hazard to maintain their rights, led our fathers to enter on the trial of revolution. Having achieved the separation, they did what was in their power for the development of commerce. They secured free trade between the States, without surrendering State independence. Their sons, not only free, but beyond the possibility of future interference in their domestic affairs, now seek the closest commercial connection with the country from which their fathers achieved a political separation.

Had the proposition been made to consolidate the States after their independence had been achieved, all must know it would have been rejected--yet there are those who now instigate you to sectional strife for the purpose of sectional dominion and the destruction of the rights of the minority. Do they mean treason to the Constitution and the destruction of the Union? Or do they vilely practice on credulity and passion for personal gain? The latter is suggested by the contradictory course they pursue. At the same time they proclaim war upon the slave property of the South, they ask for protection to the manufactures of the staple which could not be produced if that property did not exist. And while they assert themselves to be the peculiar friends of commerce and navigation, they vaunt their purpose to destroy the labor which gives vitality to both; whilst they proclaim themselves the peculiar friends of laboring men at the North, they insist that the negroes are their equals; and if they are sincere they would, by emancipation of the blacks, bring them together and degrade the white man to the negro level. They seek to influence the northern mind by sectional issues and sectional organization, yet they profess to be the friends of the Union. The Union voluntarily formed by free, equal, independent States.

We of the South, on a sectional division, are in the minority; and if legislation is to be directed by geographical tests--if the constitution is to be trampled in the dust, and the unbridled will of the majority in Congress is to be supreme over the States; we should have the problem which was presented to our Fathers when the Colonies declined to be content with a mere representation in parliament.

If the constitution is to be sacredly observed, why should there be a struggle for sectional ascendency? The instrument is the same in all latitudes, and does not vary with the domestic institutions of the several States. Hence it is that the Democracy, the party of the constitution, have preserved their integrity, and are to-day the only national party and the only hope for the preservation and perpetuation of the Union of the States.

Mr. Jefferson denominated the Democracy of the North, the natural allies of the South. It is in our generation doubly true; they are still the party with whom labor is capital, and they are now the party which stands by the barriers of the constitution, to protect them from the waves of fanatical and sectional aggression. The use of the word aggression reminded him that the people here have been daily harangued about the aggressions of the slave power, and he had been curious to learn what was so described. It is, if he had learned correctly, the assertion of the right to migrate with slaves into the territories of the United States. Is this aggression? If so, upon what? Not upon those who desire close association with the negro; not upon territorial rights, unless these self-styled lovers of the Union have already dissolved it and have taken the territories to themselves. The territory being the common property of States, equals in the Union, and bound by the constitution which recognizes property in slaves, it is an abuse of terms to call aggression the migration into that territory of one of its joint owners, because carrying with him any species of property recognized by the constitution of the United States. The Federal government has no power to declare what is property anywhere. The power of each State cannot extend beyond its own limits. As a consequence, therefore, whatever is property in any of the States must be so considered in any of the territories of the United States until they reach to the dignity of community independence, when the subject matter will be entirely under the control of the people and be determined by their fundamental law. If the inhabitants of any territory should refuse to enact such laws and police regulations as would give security to their property or to his, it would be rendered more or less valueless, in proportion to the difficulty of holding it without such protection. In the case of property in the labor of man, or what is usually called slave property, the insecurity would be so great that the owner could not ordinarily retain it. Therefore, though the right would remain, the remedy being withheld, it would follow that the owner would be practically debarred by the circumstances of the case, from taking slave property into a territory where the sense of the inhabitants was opposed to its introduction. So much for the oft repeated fallacy of forcing slavery upon any community.

If Congress had the power to prohibit the introduction of slave property into the territories, what would be the purpose? Would it be to promote emancipation? That could not be the effect. In the first settlement of a territory the want of population and the consequent difficulty of procuring hired labor, would induce emigrants to take slaves with them; but if the climate and products of the country were unsuited to African labor--as soon as white labor flowed in, the owners of slaves would as a matter of interest, desire to get rid of them and emancipation would result. The number would usually be so small that this would be effected without injury to society or industrial pursuits. Thus it was in Wisconsin, notwithstanding the ordinance of '87; and other examples might be cited to show that this is not mere theory.

Would it be to promote the civilization and progress of the negro race? The tendency must be otherwise. By the dispersion of the slaves, their labor would be rendered more productive and their comforts increased. The number of owners would be multiplied, and by more immediate contact and personal relation greater care and kindness would be engendered. In every way it would conduce to the advancement and happiness of the servile caste.

No--no--it is not these, but the same answer which comes to every inquiry as to the cause of fanatical agitation. 'Tis for sectional power, and political ascendency; to fan a sectional hostility, which must be, as it has been, injurious to all, and beneficial to none. For what patriotic purpose can the Northern mind be agitated in relation to domestic institutions, for which they have no legal or moral responsibility, and from the interference with which they are restrained by their obligations as American citizens?

Is it in this mode that the spirit of mutual support and common effort for the common good, is to be cultivated? Is it thus that confidence is to be developed and the sense of security to grow with the growing power of each and every State? Is it thus that we are to exemplify the blessings of self-government by the free exercise in each independent community of the power to regulate their domestic institutions as soil, climate, and population may determine?

Among the questions which have been made the basis of recent agitation, and has contributed as much, perhaps, as any other to popular delusion, was the act known as the Missouri Compromise. It will be remembered that the agitation of 1819 on the subject of slavery, was not masked as it has been since, by pretensions of philanthropy--it was an avowed opposition to the admission of a slave-holding State. A long and bitter controversy was terminated by the admission of the State of Missouri, and the prohibition of slavery north of the parallel of 36 deg. 30 minutes. He, and those with whom he most concurred, had always contended that Congress had no constitutional power to make the interdiction. But the people having generally acquiesced, the matter was considered settled; and when Texas, a slave-holding State, was admitted into the Union, Southern men, regarding the Missouri Act as a compact, assented to the extension of the line through the territory of Texas, with a provision that any State formed out of the territory north of 36: 30: should be non-slaveholding. But when, at a subsequent period, we made extensive acquisitions from Mexico, and it was proposed to divide the territory by the same parallel, the North generally opposed it, and after a long discussion, the controversy was settled on the principle of non-intervention by Congress in relation to property in the territories. The line of the Missouri Compromise was repudiated. And a Senator who had been most prominent in denouncing the repeal of the Missouri Compromise as a violation of good faith on the part of the South, in 1850, described it as a measure which had been the grave of every Northern man who supported it, and objected to the boundary of 36: 30: for the territory of Utah, because of the political implication which its adoption would contain.

The act having been thus signally repudiated by the denial in every form of the power of Congress to fix geographical limits within which slavery might or might not exist; when it became necessary to organize the territories of Kansas and Nebraska, it was but the corollary of the proposition which had been maintained in 1850 to repeal the act which had fixed the parallel of 36: 30: as the future limit of slavery in the territory of Louisiana.

Consistency demanded so much; fairness and manhood could not have granted less. He was not then a member of Congress; but if he had been, he should have voted for that repeal; for although in 1850 he had favored the extension of the Missouri Compromise line to the Pacific Ocean, and believed that it would most conduce to the harmony of the States, he had yielded to the action of the Government, and considered the position then taken as conclusive against the retention of the line in Louisiana and Texas, which its beneficiaries had refused to extend through the territories acquired from Mexico. As a general principle, he thought it was best to leave the territories all open. Equality of right demanded it, and the federal government had no power to withhold it. Whatever validity the

Missouri Compromise act had, it derived from the acquiescence of the people. After 1850 then it had none. The South had not asked Congress to extend slavery into the territories, and he in common with most Southern statesmen, denied the existence of any power to do so. He held it to be the creed of the Democracy, both in the North and the South, that the General Government had no constitutional power either to establish or prohibit slavery anywhere; a grant of power to do the one must necessarily have involved the power to do the other. Hence it is their policy not to interfere on the one side or the other, but protecting each individual in his constitutional rights, to leave every independent community to determine and adjust all domestic questions as in their wisdom may seem best.

Politicians of the opposite school seemed to forget the relation of the General Government to the States; even so far as to argue as though the General Government had been the creator instead of the creature of the States. He had learned that attempts had been made to impress upon the people of Maine the belief that they were in danger of having slavery established among them by decree of the Supreme Court of the United States. He scarcely knew how to answer so palpable an absurdity. The court was established, among other purposes, to protect the people from unconstitutional legislation; and if Congress, in the extreme of madness, should attempt thus to invade the sovereignty of a State, it would be within the power, and would be the duty of the court, to check the aggression by declaring such law void. The court have, on more than one occasion, asserted the right of transit as a consequence of the guarantees of the Constitution, but it would require much ingenuity to torture the protection of a traveller or sojourner into an assertion of a right to become resident and introduce property in contravention of the fundamental law of the State, or of a citizen to hold property within a State in violation of its constitution and its policy. The error of the proposition was so palpable that, like the truth of an axiom, it could not be rendered plainer by demonstration.

It is not within the scope of human foresight to see the embarrassments which may arise in the execution of any policy. When it was declared that soil, climate, and unrestrained migration should be left to fix the status of the territories, and institutions of the States to be formed out of them, no one probably anticipated that companies would be incorporated to transport colonists into a territory with a view to decide its political condition. Congress, as he believed, yielding too far to the popular idea, had surrendered its right of revision and thus had recently lost its power to restrain improper legislation in the territories. From these joint causes had arisen the unhappy strife in Kansas, which at one time threatened to terminate in civil war. The Government had been denounced for the employment of United States troops. Very briefly he would state the case.

The movement of the Emigrant Aid Societies of the North was met by counteracting movements in Missouri and other Southern States. Thus opposing tides of emigration met on the plains of Kansas. The land was a scene of confusion and violence. Fortunately the murders which for a time filled the newspapers, existed nowhere else; and the men who were reported slain, usually turned up after a short period to enjoy the eulogies which their martyrdom had elicited. But arson, theft and disgraceful scenes of disorder did really exist, and bands of armed men indicated the approach of actual hostilities. What was the Government to do? Perhaps you will say, call out the militia. But that would have been to feed and arm one of the parties for the destruction of the other. To call out the militia of neighboring States would have been but little better. The sectional excitement then ran so high, that they would probably have met upon the fields of Kansas as combatants, the government in the meantime furnishing the supplies for both armies. It was necessary to have a force--one which would be free from sectional excitement or partisan zeal and under executive control. The army fulfiled these conditions. It was therefore employed. It dispersed marauding parties, disarmed organized invaders, arrested disturbers of the peace, gave comparative quiet and repose to the territory, without taking a single life, aye, or shedding one drop of blood. The end justified the means, and the result equaled all that could have been anticipated.

The anomalous condition of a territory possessing full legislative power, but not invested with the sovereignty of a State, justified the anxiety exhibited by Congress to be relieved from the embarrassment which the case of Kansas presented. The Senate passed a bill to authorize a convention for the preparation of a constitution for the admission of Kansas as a State. It however failed in the House of Representatives, and the legislature of Kansas, availing themselves of the plenary power conferred upon them by the organic act, proceeded to provide for the assembling of a convention, and the formation of a constitution. The law was minute and fair in its provisions, so nearly resembling the bill of the Senate that the one was probably copied from the other. It seemed to secure to every legal voter every desirable opportunity to exercise his right. One of the parties of the territory, however, denying the legal existence of the legislature, chose to abstain from voting. The other elected the delegates who formed the constitution. The validity of the instrument he has been denied, because it was not submitted for popular ratification. He held this position to be wholly untenable, and could but regard it as a gross departure from the principle of popular sovereignty. A people--he used the word in its strict political sense--having the right to make for themselves their fundamental law, may either assemble in mass convention for that purpose, or may select delegates and limit their power to the preparation of an instrument to be submitted to a popular decision; or they may appoint delegates with full powers to frame the fundamental law of the land. Whether they adopt one mode or the other is a question with which others have no right to interfere, and he who claims for Congress the power to sit in judgment on the manner in which a people may form a constitution, is outside of the barrier which would restrain him from claiming for Congress the right to dictate the instrument itself. If the right existed to form a constitution at all, the power of Congress in relation to the instrument was limited to the simple inquiry: is it republican? In this view of the case it would not matter to him the ninety-ninth part of a hair whether a people should chose to admit or exclude slave property. Their right to enter the Union would be a thing apart from that consideration.

He had felt great doubt as to the propriety of admitting Kansas, and had only yielded those doubts to the peculiar necessities which seemed to make the case exceptional. The inhabitants of the territory had however decided not to enter the Union upon the terms proposed, and he thought their decision was fortunate. They had not the requisite population; their resources were too limited to give assurance that they would be able to bear the expenses of their government and properly to perform the duties of a State. But more than this, their legislative history shows that they are wanting in the essential characteristics of a community; whichever party has had the control of the legislature, has manifested by its acts not a desire to promote the public good, and protect individual rights, but a purpose to war upon their political opponents as a hostile power. The political party with which he most sympathized had marked its legislation by requiring test oaths, offensive to all our notions of political freedom; and the other party had assumed to take from the territorial executive the control of the militia and to place it in irresponsible hands, where, it reports speak truly, it has been employed in the most wanton outrages and disgraceful persecution of citizens of the opposite political party. He held, therefore, that the decision of the inhabitants was fortunate and wise. It was well, that before they assume the responsibilities of a State, they should gather population, develop the natural resources of the country, and above all acquire the homogeneous character which would give security to person and property, and fit them to be justly denominated a community.

A stranger, and but a passing observer of events in Maine, he had nevertheless seen indications of a reaction in popular opinion, which promised hopefully for the future of Democracy, hopefully, it might be permitted for one to say who believed that the success of the Democracy was the only hope for the maintenance of the constitution and the perpetuation of the Union which sprung from and cannot outlive it. If the language of his friend who preceded him should prove prophetic, the waving of the banner he described would be the dawning of a day which would bring gladness and confidence to many a heart now clouded with distrust, and loud would be the cheers which, on distant plain and mountain, would welcome Maine again to her position on the top of the Democratic pyramid. He saw a brighter sky above him; he felt a firmer foundation beneath his feet, and hoped ere long through a triumph achieved by the declaration of principles, suited to every latitude and longitude of the United Slates, to receive the assurance that we have passed the breakers --that our ship may henceforth float freely on--that our flag, no longer threatened with mutilation or destruction, shall throw its broad stripes to the breeze and gather stars until its constellation shines a galaxy, and records a family of States embracing the new world and its adjacent islands.

SPEECH AT STATE FAIR AT AUGUSTA, ME

[From the Eastern Argus, Sept 29,1858.]

ON Thursday evening a large and brilliant audience assembled in the Representatives' Hall, in the Capitol, to listen to the distinguished statesman from Mississippi, who, upon brief notice and without a moment's leisure for preparation, had kindly consented to address the Agricultural Society. We have already spoken of the gratifying character of what he termed his desultory remarks and of the cordially enthusiastic manner in which both the orator and his address were received. As the occasion, as well as the character of the remarks, will make them interesting to the whole people of our State, we are gratified in being able to lay before our readers a more extended and accurate report of them than has before appeared.

At about half-past eight o'clock, the Society came into the Hall, already crowded in every part, and its President, Hon. Samuel F. Perley, in brief and complimentary terms, introduced Col. Davis, who advanced to the speaker's stand, and was received with loud and prolonged applause. He said:

Ladies and gentlemen, friends and countrymen: To the many acts of kindness received from the people of Maine, I have to add the welcome reception this evening. The invitation of the Agricultural Society, with the attendant circumstances, serve further to impress me with the hospitality of ray fellow citizens of this State. Coming here, an invalid, seeking the benefits which your clime would afford, and preceded by a reputation which was expected to prejudice you unfavorably towards me, I have everywhere met courtesy and considerate attention, from the hour I landed on your coast to the present time. It was natural to ask, whence come these manifestations? Is it because the opinion which had been formed has been found to be unjust, and the reaction has been in proportion to the previous impulse? Or is it the exhibition of your regard for loyalty to one's friends, and devotion by a citizen to the community to which he belongs? Either the one or the other is honorable to you; but there is a broader and more beneficent motive--the prompting of that sentiment which would cause you to recognize in every American citizen a brother. That feeling which Daniel Webster indicated when he met me in company with your distinguished townsman, ex-Senator Bradbury, and taking us with the right hand and with the left, said in the peculiarly impressive manner which belonged to him, "My brethren of the North and of the South, how are ye?"

It is usual to offer to an Agricultural Society nothing less than a prepared address, and had I come with an intention to speak to you, I should not have failed to make that preparation which is evidence of due regard for the audience. The invitation under which I now speak, having been given and accepted this evening, I have no power to do more than to offer you desultory remarks on such subjects as my visit to the Fair have suggested, and which may occur to me as I progress.

With great pleasure I have witnessed evidences of much attention and deep interest in agriculture. It is the basis of all wealth. It is the producer--brings all new contributions to the general store. The mechanic arts are essential to its success, and they serve by changing the form, to multiply the value of agricultural products. And commerce too, by exchanging the products of individuals and of countries, enhances the value of labor, and increases the comfort of man. They are all essential to each other. I have no disposition to magnify or depreciate either, but my proposition is, that the soil is the source from which human wealth springs. In addition to these pursuits, society requires what are termed liberal professions. They are not producers, though they may contribute, by diffusing knowledge, to increase production. They may be necessary to give security to property and to take care of some physical wants. For instance you have lawyers and doctors; and the less need you have of them the better; for though necessary, like government, it is evil which makes them so. As to another class--those who have the cure of souls--their mission is so sacred, their function so high as to place them beyond comment; and of them I have nothing to say, except that I propose to say nothing.

Among the products of agriculture I of course intended to include the farmer's stock, and I must here bear my tribute of admiration to the fine display which has been made of horned cattle; particularly of work oxen, remarkable for their size, their adaptation to the purposes for which they are kept and the docility and yet the unflagging spirit which they manifested in the trials of strength and of deep ploughing. I have not before seen such fine specimens of the Devon cattle,--of course I speak of them as they present themselves to the eye--not pretending to judge of their relative value to other stock exhibited. Improvement in the breed of domestic animals goes hand in hand with agricultural mechanism, to give the ability to make two blades of grass to grow where but one grew before, and thus to render you indeed benefactors. Skill in the use, and ingenuity in devising and constructing implements, serve to render labor productive, and relieve it of its most dreary drudgery. It is this mechanical ingenuity which has compensated for the high price of labor among us, and aided in the development of resources which makes our country the greatest of the earth. Blest by soil, climate and government, if we are, as claimed, pre-eminent among nations, it is because we have added to other advantages a more general cultivation of the mind. The superiority is attributable not so much to physical energy, activity and perseverance, as to the improvement of that portion of the man which lies above the eyes.

Though you have done much for the improvement of agricultural implements, your work is far from being completed. It is not a little surprising that we should, to this day, have no reliable rule by which to make a plough, and though the model has been improved, certainly it is yet not unlike, and so far as exact science is concerned, is on a par with that implement as used by the Romans, and as it appeared in ancient architecture; the form, proportion and angular relation of the parts, and the adjustment of the whole to the power to be applied, offer problems alike interesting to the mechanic, and useful to the cultivator. In your ploughing matches sufficient evidence was afforded of the fitness of the implements employed to turn deep and wide furrows; but should we be content with such result as is obtained by trying different models, and then copying one which is found to be good?

Maine was so richly endowed with harbors and forests of ship timber that it was naturally to be expected, as it has fallen out, that the pursuits of navigation would most occupy the attention of her people. But let not her sons look to the period when her forests have disappeared as that beyond which her prosperity may not continue. There are large tracts of land which when labor is no longer directed to lumber, will become, in the hands of the farmer, what the valley of the Kennebec now is. The land may not offer soil so deep as alluvial districts, nor be at first as productive as those on which a deep vegetable mould has accumulated, yet its productiveness may not be less permanent than those. In them the elements which support the farmer's crop may be exhausted by cultivation or carried down into substrata of gravel or sand. In the remote West to which so many are pressing, the emigrant will encounter an arid climate in which irrigation is necessary to ensure a return for the labor of husbandry, and this involves an original expenditure which it will usually require large capital to bear. In this climate the sun, like a mighty pump, is daily raising the water which the currents of cold air from the mountains, or from the sea, precipitate in the form of genial showers during the period of your growing crops; and the granite of the mountains slowly, but steadily disintegrating, gives up its fertilizing property to be scattered by unseen hands over plain and over valley. With care and with skill in its use I can see no end to the productiveness of that portion of your land which is fit for cultivation.

Your crops, and your mode of tillage are different from that to which I am accustomed, and the result is that each supplies a different segment in the circle of man's wants. I am glad that it is so, that it must necessarily be so. Glad, because it is an everlasting bond between us; one which, whilst it binds, renders both doubly prosperous. Blessed is our lot in this, that our fathers linked us together, and established free trade between us. In the diversity of climate, and of crops, there is an assurance that entire failure cannot occur. If disaster and blight should fall upon one section, it need not go to a foreign land in search of bread. Famine, gaunt famine, with its skeleton step, can never pass our borders whilst the free trade of the Union continues.

But difference in pursuits, in population, and domestic institutions, have been made the basis of hostile agitation, and urged as a cause of separation. To my mind the reverse would be the rational conclusion. Each exchanging, the surplus of that which it can best produce for the surplus of another which it most requires, the benefit must be mutual, and the advantage common. Here is a commercial, a selfish bond to hold us together. But I will stop here, because the current of my thought is carrying me beyond the limit of topics proper to the occasion, and I must offer as an apology the fact, that though myself a cultivator of the soil, my mind has for several years been given so much to political subjects, that in speaking without having previously arranged what to say, the thought inadvertently runs from the matter I wished to present, into collateral questions of governmental concern. Before turning back, however, into the original channel, permit me to say that the diversity of which I have been speaking, formed no small inducement to the union of the States, and that it has been through that union that we have attained to our present position, and stand to-day, all things considered, the happiest, and among the greatest in the family of nations.

In looking around upon the evidences you have brought of mechanical and agricultural improvement, I have viewed it not with the curiosity of a stranger, but with the interest of one who felt that he had a part in it, as an exhibition of the prosperity of his country. The whole confederacy is my country, and to the innermost fibres of my heart I love it all, and every part. I could not if I would, and would not if I could, dwarf myself to mere sectionality. My first allegiance is to the State of which I am a citizen, and to which by affection and association I am personally bound; but this does not obstruct the perception of your greatness, or admiration for much which I have found admirable among you.

Yankee is a word once applied to you as a term of reproach, but you have made it honorable and renowned. You have borne the flag of your country from the time when it was ridiculed as a piece of striped bunting, until it has come to be known and respected wherever the ray of civilization has reached; and your canvass-winged birds of commerce have borne civilization into regions, where it is not boasting to say, but for your prowess it would not have gone. You have a right to be proud of your achievements as well on the land as the sea. Well may you point as you do with satisfaction, to your school houses and your work-shops, and to the fruits they have borne on the forum and in the council chamber, and in the manufactures which have increased the comforts of our own people, and have encircled the globe to find exchangeable products required at home. Those are the greatest and most beneficent triumphs--the triumph of mind over matter. These are the monuments of greatness, which resist both time and circumstance.

I have spoken of diversity among the people of the United States; yet there is probably greater similitude than is to be found elsewhere over the same extent of country, and in the same number of people. In language, especially, our people are one; surely much more so than those of any other country. The diversity between the people of the different States, even those most remote from each other, is not as great as that between inhabitants of adjoining countries of England, or departments of France or Spain, where provinces have their separate dialects. And chief among the causes for this I would place the primary book, in which children of my day learned their letters, and took their first lessons in spelling and reading. I refer to the good old spelling book of Noah Webster, on which I doubt if there has been any improvement, and which had the singular advantage of being used over the whole country. To this unity of language and general similitude, is to be added a community of sentiment wherever the American is brought into contrast or opposition to any other people.

If shadows float over our disc and threaten an eclipse; if there be those who would not avert, but desire to precipitate catastrophe to the Union, these are not the sentiments of the American heart; they are rather the exceptions and should not disturb our confidence in that deep-seated sentiment of nationality which aided our fathers when they entered into the compact of union, and which has preserved it to us. You manifest that sentiment to-day in the courtesy which you have extended to me. In what other land could a countryman go so far from his home and receive among strangers the attention which could only be expected from friends? But it is not your kindness only, which has caused me here to feel at home; I have been brought in contact with men of my own pursuit, the tillers of the ground and the breeders of stock; and in my intercourse with this class of your citizens, I have been further confirmed in the high estimate heretofore placed upon that portion of our population. Happily for our country and its institutions, extensive territory and favorable climate, have attracted a large part of our population to agricultural pursuits. It is in the individuality, the sobriety, and self reliance of the rural population that I look for the highest development of those qualities essential to self-government, and the brightest illustration of patriotic devotion. They may not be the best informed, but learning and wisdom are by no means equivalent terms. Isolation and entire dependence upon himself; give independence of character and favor that self-inquiry which best enables man to comprehend and measure the motives of his fellow. Crowded together in cities originality is lost, mind becomes as it were acadamized; and though the intercourse is favorable to the acquisition of knowledge, it is most unfriendly to that individuality, independence, and purity, without which republican governments rapidly sink into decay. It was probably in this view that Mr. Jefferson said, great cities were sores upon the body politic. Needful for the purposes of commerce, required for the exchanges on which agricultural and manufacturing industry depend for their prosperity,--they are not evils which we could desire to see abated. My desire, however, is, that the rural districts shall not lose their relative importance or cease to control in public affairs. Misled and deceived they may be, interested in a public wrong they cannot be, and theirs is the sober thought upon which reliance must be placed for the correction of errors and delusions, which may temporarily prevail.

In societies like this the farmers have the opportunity of comparing opinions and results, and thus increasing the amount of their knowledge. The spirit of emulation which is excited must lead to improvement, by better directing energy in their pursuit. The publication of the results and the comparisons thus instituted with what is done in other States, encourages State pride and developes community feeling. Whatever tends to the cultivation of the idea of State sovereignty and community independence, strengthens the foundation on which rests our federal government--the fruition of that principle which led our fathers into the war of the revolution, where they purchased with their blood the rich inheritance transmitted to us.

Man once received the title of Domitor Equi, he being proud of the achievement of taming the horse, and then, so far as we can learn, gentler woman sat like Penelope handling the distaff. Subsequently there arose a race of Amazons, who, aspiring to the feats of man, lost the gentleness of woman; but in our happy land and day, rising above the one without running to the excess of the other, lovely woman, with all the gentle charms which graced a Penelope, musters her energy when occasion requires, and displays her prowess in commanding the horse. Among the interesting features of the exhibition I shall remember the equestrianism of the ladies. Though it was beautiful in every sense of the word, it was not regarded as mere sport, but the rather looked upon as part of that mental and physical training which makes a woman more than the mere ornament of the drawing-room--fits her usefully to act her appropriate part in the trying scenes to which the most favored may be subjected--to become the mother of heroes, and live in the admiration of posterity.

Fears had once been entertained and much opposition was formerly made to an extension of the area of the United States. A wiser policy, however, prevailed, and the introduction of new regions, increasing the variety of our productions, have magnified the advantages of free trade between the States, and made us almost independent of other countries for the supply of every object whether of necessity or of luxury. I would be glad to extend our boundary and make the circle of our products complete, so that, whilst we would encourage commerce with christendom we should be, commercially as we are politically, absolutely independent, whenever it should be proper or necessary to terminate intercourse with any or every other country. A statesman of former days wished that the Atlantic was a sea of fire, that it might be a barrier to shut out European contamination. Whatever fear was once justifiable, no apprehension now need to exist, that our people will imitate or seek to adopt the political theories of Europe. We have recently rejoiced in the success of the attempt to establish telegraphic communication with England; because in closer commercial ties we saw no danger of political influence. I was happy this evening to receive assurances that the success of that enterprise was at last complete. I have not been of those whose doubts were stronger than their hopes--thanks to a sanguine temperament. I have from the beginning anticipated success, and have heretofore said that if the present attempt riled I was sure that Yankee enterprise and skill could make a cable and lay it across the Atlantic. And we look forward to the result with hope, not doubting, that the closest commercial connexion with other countries can only bring to us benefits. We are not, and have not been, political propagandists, yet believing our form of government the best, we properly desire its extension and invite the world to scrutinize our example of representative liberty.

The stars on our flag, recording the number of the States united, have already been more than doubled; and I hopefully look forward to the day when the constellation shall become a galaxy covering the stripes, which record the original number of our political family, and shall shed over the nations of the earth the light of regeneration to mankind. It has sometimes been said to he our manifest destiny that we should possess the whole of this continent. Whether it shall ever all be part of the United States is doubtful, and may never be desirable; but that in some form or other, it should come under the protectorate or control of the United States, is a result which seems to me, in the remote future, certain. It waits as the consequence upon intellectual vigor, upon physical energy, upon the capacity to govern, and can only be defeated by a suicidal madness, of which it does not belong to the occasion to treat.

I would not be understood to advocate what is called fillibustering. Our country has never obtained territory except fairly, honorably and peaceably. We have conquered territory, but have asserted no title as the right of conquest, returning to Mexico all except the part she agreed to sell and for which we paid a liberal price. England having fillibustered around the world, has reproached us for aggrandizement, and we point to history and invite a comparison. There is no stain upon our escutcheon, no smoke upon our garments, and thus may they remain pure forever! The acquisitions of which I spoke, the protectorate which was contemplated, were such as the necessities of the future should demand, and the good of others as much as our own require, and this step by step, faster or slower, will, I believe, finally embrace the continent of America and its adjacent islands.

I am not among those who desire to incorporate into our Union, countries densely populated with a different race. Deserts, 'tis the province of our people to subdue. A mere handful of inhabitants, such as existed in Louisiana, are soon enveloped in the tide of immigration; of this character of acquisition I have no fear; but the mingling of races is a different thing. I have looked with interest and pleasure upon the crosses of your cattle and horses, and saw in it the evidence of improvement. Let your Messengers, your Morgans, your Drews, and your Eatons be mingled with each other and with new inportations; so with your Durhams, Devons, Ayreshires and your Jerseys. The limit to these experiments will be where experience shows deterioration. There is one cross which it is to be hoped you will avoid: 'tis that which your Puritan fathers would not adopt or even entertain. They kept pure the Caucasian blood which flowed in their veins, and therein is the cause of your present high civilization, your progress, your dignity and your strength. We are one, let us remain unmixed. In our neighbors of Southern and Central America we have a sufficient warning; and may it never be our ill-fortune to learn by experience the lessons taught by their example.

It is due to the hospitality and kind consideration with which I have been treated since I first came among you that I should not leave you under any doubt in relation to the accusations which have been busily circulated against me. And this, it is to be hoped, will not be mistaken for egotism, since the greatest interest I have in doing so is to justify you to yourselves. I know of no selfish purpose, unless a proper desire for esteem he such, which would lead me to attempt to undeceive you, so far as any of you may have been imposed upon. I certainly do not expect to change my residence from the State in which I was reared;

and I long since avowed the intention never again to receive official trust from any other authority than that of the people of the State of which I am a citizen. It has been represented to you that you were showering attentions upon one who was hostile to your interests, and regardless of your rights. I am grateful to you for the constant evidence you have given that you discredited the statement, and I am therefore the more anxious that you should not remain in doubt. The public record contains all I have said and done, and in it nothing can be found to sustain the statement. Of this I am quite sure, because it has always been with me a principle to exercise public functions in the spirit of the Constitution and the purposes of the Union. If I know myself, I have never given a vote from a feeling of hostility to any portion of our common country; but have always kept in view the common obligation for the common welfare, and desired by maintaining the constitution in each and every particular, to perpetuate the blessings it was designed to secure, and to transmit the inheritance received from our fathers unmutilated and uncontaminated to remotest posterity. In some positions it has devolved upon me to study interests in Maine, with a view to secure for them proper provision, and I feel that I am justified in saying they were considered as became one who had sworn to protect the Constitution, and who had a function to perform in relation to a sovereign State of the Union. Heretofore I have been prompted merely by what I believed to be duty to you from me as an officer under the Constitution. Hereafter, though the principles on which I will act cannot vary, I should be less than a man if I did not feel deeper interest in whatever concerns you. I shall always bear with me most pleasurable recollections of my sojourn among you, and hope it may be my good fortune some day to meet some of you in Mississippi, and thus have it in my power to reciprocate, imperfectly it may be, the kindness which you bestowed upon me. I thank you for your polite attention, and cordially wish for you, one and all, present and future prosperity.

SPEECH AT THE GRAND RATIFICATION MEETING, FANEUIL HALL

Monday evening, Oct. 11th, 1858

COUNTRYMEN, Brethren, Democrats--Most happy am I to meet you, and to have received here renewed assurance--of that which I have so long believed--that the pulsationof the democratic heart is the same in every parallel of latitude, on every meridian of longitude throughout the United States. But it required not this to confirm me in a belief so long and so happily enjoyed.--Your own great statesman who has introduced me to this assembly has been too long associated with me, too nearly connected, we have labored too many hours, sometimes even until one day ran into another, in the cause of our country, for me to than to understand that a Massachusetts democrat has a heart comprehending the whole of our wide Union, and that its pulsations always beat for the liberty and happiness of its country. Neither could I be unaware such was the sentiment of the democracy of New England. For it was lay fortune lately to serve under a President drawn from the neighboring, State of New Hampshire, [applause,] and I know that he spoke the language of his heart, for I learned it in tour years of intimate connection with him, when he said he knew "no north, no south, no east, no west, but sacred maintenance of the common bond and true devotion to the common brotherhood." Never, sir, in the past history of our country, never, I add, in its future destiny, however bright it may be, did or will a man of higher and purer patriotism, a man more devoted to the common weal of his country, hold the helm of our great ship of State, than that same New Englander, Franklin Pierce. [Applause.]

I have heard the resolutions read and approved by this meeting; heard the address of your candidate for Governor; and these added to the address of my old and intimate friend, Gen. Cushing, bear to me fresh testimony, which I shall be happy to carry away with me, that the democracy, in the language of your own glorious Webster, "still lives," lives not as his great spirit did, when it hung 'twixt life and death, like a star upon the horizon's verge, but lives like the germ that is shooting upward, like the sapling that is growing to a mighty tree, the branches of which will spread over the commonwealth, and may redeem and restore Massachusetts to her once glorious place in the Union.

As I look around me and see this venerable hall thus thronged, it reminds me of another meeting, when it was found too small to contain the assembly--that great meeting which assembled here, when the people were called upon to decide what should be done in relation to the tea-tax. Faneuil Hall, on that occasion, was found too small, and the people went to the Old South Church, which still stands--a monument of your early history. And I hope the day will soon come when many Democratic meetings in Boston will be too large for Faneuil Hall! [Applause.] I am welcomed to this hall, so venerable for its associations with our early history; to this hall of which you are so justly proud, and the memories of which are part of the inheritance of every American citizen; and feel, as I remember how many voices of patriotic fervor have here been heard; that in it originated the first movements from which the Revolution sprung; that here began that system of town meetings and free discussion which is the glory and safety of our country; that I had enough to warn me, that though my theme was more humble than theirs, (as befitted my poorer ability,) that it was a hazardous thing for me to attempt to speak in this sacred temple. But when I heard your statesman (Gen. Cushing) say, that a word once here spoken never dies, that it becomes a part of the circumambient air, I felt a reluctance to speak which increases upon me as I recall his expression. But if those voices which breathed the first instincts into the Colony of Massachusetts, and into those colonies which formed the United States, to proclaim community independence, and asserts it against the powerful mother country, --if those voices live here still, how must they feel who come here to preach treason to the Constitution, and assail the Union it ordained and established? [Applause.] It would seem that their criminal hearts should fear that those voices, so long slumbering, would break their silence, that the forms which look down from these walls behind and around me, would walk forth. and that their sabres would once more be drawn from their scabbards, to drive from this sacred temple fanatical men, who desecrate it more than did the changers of money and those who sold doves, the temple of the living God. [Loud cheers.]

And here, too, you have, to remind you, and to remind all who enter this hall, the portraits of those men who are dear to every lover of liberty, and part and parcel of the memory of every American citizen. Highest among them all I see you have placed Samuel Adams and John Hancock. [Applause.] You have placed them the highest and properly; for they were the two, the only two, excepted from the proclamation of mercy, when Governor Gage issued his anathema against them and their fellow patriots. These men, thus excepted from the saving grace of the crown, now occupy the highest place in Faneuil Hall, and thus are consecrated highest in the reverence of the people of Boston. [Applause.] This is one of the instances in which we find tradition more reliable than history; for tradition has borne the name of Samuel Adams to the remotest corner of our territory, placed it among the household words taught to the rising generation, and there in the new States intertwined with our love of representative liberty, it is a name as sacred among us as it is among you of New England. [Applause.]

We remember how early he saw the necessity of community independence. How, through the dim mists of the future, and in advance of his day, he looked forward to the proclamation of that independence by Massachusetts; how he steadily strove, through good report and evil report, with the same unwavering purpose, whether in the midst of his fellow citizens, cheered by their voices, or whether isolated, a refugee, hunted as a criminal, and communing with his own heart, now under all circumstances his eve was still fixed upon his first, last hope, the community independence of Massachusetts! And when we see him, at a later period, the leader in that correspondence which waked the feelings of the other colonies and brought into fraternal association the people of Massachusetts with the people of other colonies--when we see his letters acknowledging the receipt of the rice of South Carolina, the flour, the pork, the money of Virginia, Maryland, New York, Pennsylvania, and others, contributions of affection to relieve Boston of the sufferings inflicted upon her when her port was closed by the despotism of the British crown--we there see the beginning of that sentiment which insured the co-operation of the colonies throughout the desperate struggle of the Revolution, and which, if the present generation be true to the compact of their sires, to the memory and to the principles of the noble men from whom they descended, will perpetuate for them that spirit of fraternity in which the Union began. [Applause.]

But it is not here alone, nor in reminiscences connected with the objects which present themselves within this hall, that the people of Boston have much to excite their patriotism and carry them back to the great principles of the revolutionary struggle.

Where in this vicinity will you go and not meet some monument to inspire such sentiments? On one side are Lexington and Concord, where sixty brave countrymen came with their fowling pieces to oppose six hundred veterans,--where peaceful citizens animated by the love of independence and covered by the triple shield of a righteous cause, finally forced those veterans back, and pursued them on the road, fighting from every barn and bush, and stock, and stone, till they drove them to the shelters from which they had gone forth! [Applause.] And there on another side of your city stand those monuments of your early patriotism, Breed's and Bunker's Hill whose soil drank the sacred blood of men who lived for their country and died for mankind! Can it be that any of you tread that soil and forget the great purposes for which those men bravely fought, or nobly died?" [Applause.] While in yet another direction rise the Heights of Dorchester, once the encampment of the great Virginian, the man who came here in the cause of American independence, who did not ask "Is this a town of Virginia?" but, "Is this a town of my brethren?" who pitched his camp and commenced his operations with the steady courage and cautious wisdom characteristic of Washington, hopefully, resolutely waiting and watching for the day when he could drive the British troops out of your city. [Cheers.]

Here, too, you find where once the Old Liberty Tree, connected with so many of your memories, grew. You ask your legend, and learn that it was cut down for firewood by the British soldiers, as some of your meeting houses were pulled down. They burned the old tree, and it warmed the soldiers enough to enable them to evacuate the city. [Laughter.] Had they been more slowly warmed into motion, had it burned a little longer, it might have lighted Washington and his followers to their enemies.

But they were gone, and never again may a hostile foe tread your shore. Woe to the enemy who shall set his footprint upon your soil; he comes to a prison or he comes to a grave! [Applause.] American fortifications are not intended to protect our country from invasion. They are constructed elsewhere as in your harbor to guard points where marine attacks can he made; and for the rest, the breasts of Americans are our parapets. [Applause.]

But, my friends, it is not merely in these military associations, so honorably connected with the pride of Massachusetts, that one who visits Boston finds much for gratification. If I were selecting a place where the advocate of strict construction of the Constitution, the extreme asserter of democratic state rights doctrine should go for his text, I would send him into the collections of your historical association. Instead of finding Boston a place where the records would teach only federalism, he would find here, in bounteous store, that sacred doctrine of state rights, which has been called the extreme and ultra opinion of the South. He would find among your early records that at the time when Massachusetts was under a colonial government, administered by a man appointed by the British crown, guarded by British soldiers; the use of this old Faneuil Hall was refused by the town authorities to a British Governor, to hold a British festival, because he was going to bring with him the agents for collecting, and naval officers sent here to enforce, an unconstitutional tax upon your commonwealth. Such was the proud spirit of independence manifested even in your colonial history. Such the great stone your fathers hewed with sturdy hand, and left the fit foundation for a monument to state rights! [Applause.] And so throughout the early period of our country you find Massachusetts leading, most prominent of all the States, in the assertion of that doctrine which has been recently so much decried.

Having achieved your independence, having passed through the confederation, you assented to the formation of our present constitutional Union. You did not surrender your state sovereignty. Your fathers had sacrificed too much to claim as the reward of their trials that they should merely have a change of masters. And a change of masters it would have been had Massachusetts surrendered her State sovereignty to the central government, and consented that that central government should have the power to coerce a State. But if this power does not exist, if this sovereignty has not been surrendered, then, I say, who can deny the words of soberness and truth spoken by your candidate this evening, when he has plead to you the cause of State independence, and the right of every community to he the judge of its own domestic affairs? [Applause.] This is all we have ever asked--we of the South, I mean,--for I stand before you one of those who have been called the ultra men of the South, and I speak, therefore, for that class; and tell you that your candidate for Governor has asserted to-night everything which we have claimed as a right, and demanded as a duty resulting from the guarantees of the Constitution, made for our mutual protection. [Applause.] Nor is here alone in that such doctrine is asserted, the like it has been my happiness to hear in your daughter, the neighboring State of Maine. I have found that the democrats there asserted the same broad, constitutional principle for which we have been contending, by which we are willing to live, for which we are willing to die! [Loud cheers and cries of "good!"]

In this state of the case, my friends, why is the country agitated? What is there practical or rational in the present excitement? Why, since the old controversies, with all their lights and shadows, have passed away, is the political firmament covered by one dark pall, the funeral shade of which increases with every passing year?

Why is it, I say, that you are thus agitated in relation to the domestic affairs of other communities? Why is it that the peace of the country is disturbed in order that one people may assume to judge of what another people should do? Is there any political power to authorize such interference? If so, where is it? You did not surrender your sovereignty. You gave to the federal government certain functions. It was your agent, created for specified purposes. It can do nothing save that which you have given it power to perform. Where is the grant of the Constitution which confers on the federal government a right to determine what shall be property? Surely none such exists; that question it belongs to every community to settle for itself: you judge in your case; every other State must judge in its case. The federal government has no power to create or establish; more palpably still, it has no power to destroy property. Do you pay taxes to an agent that he may destroy your property? Do you support him for that purpose? It is an absurdity on the face of it. To ask the question is to answer it. The government is instituted to protect, not to destroy property. In abundance of caution, your fathers provided that the federal government should not take private property, even for its own use, unless by making due compensation therefore. One of its great purposes was to increase the security of property, and by a more perfect union of forces, to render more effective protection to the States. When that power for protection becomes a source of danger, the purpose for which the government was formed will have been defeated, and the government can no longer answer the ends for which it was established.

Why, then, in the absence of all control over the subject of African slavery, are you agitated in relation to it? With Pharisaical pretension it is sometimes said it is a moral obligation to agitate, and I suppose they are going through a sort of vicarious repentance for other men's sins. [Laughter.] Who gave them a right to decide that it is a sin? By what standard do they measure it? Not the Constitution; the Constitution recognizes the property in many forms, and imposes obligations in connection with that recognition. Not the Bible; that justifies it. Not the good of society; for if they go where it exists, they find that society recognizes it as good. What, then, is their standard? The good of mankind? Is that seen in the diminished resources of the country? Is that seen in the diminished comfort of the world? Or is not the reverse exhibited? Is it in the cause of Christianity? It cannot be, for servitude is the only agency through which Christianity has reached that degraded race, the only means by which they have been civilized and elevated. Or is their charity manifested in denunciation of their brethren who are restrained from answering by the contempt which they feel for a mere brawler, whose weapons are empty words? [Applause.]

What, my friends, must be the consequences of this agitation? Good or evil? They have been evil, and evil they must be only, to the end. Not one particle of good has been done to any man, of any color, by this agitation. It has been insidiously working the purpose of sedition, for the destruction of that Union on which our hopes of future greatness depend.

On the one side, then you see agitation, tending slowly and steadily to that separation of the states, which, if you have any hope connected with the liberty of mankind, if you have any national pride in making your country the greatest of the earth, if you have any sacred regard for the obligation which the acts of your fathers entailed upon you,--by each and all of these motives you are prompted to united and earnest effort to promote the success of that great experiment which your fathers left it to you to conclude. [Applause.] On the other hand, if each community, in accordance with the principles of our government, whilst controlling its own domestic institutions, faithfully struggles as a part of the united whole, for the common benefit of all, the future points us to fraternity, to unity, to co-operation, to the increase of our own happiness, to the extension of our useful example over mankind, and the covering of that flag, whose stars have already more than doubled their original number, [applause,] with a galaxy to light the ample folds which then shall wave either the recognized flag of every state, or the recognized protector of every state upon the continent of America. [Applause.]

In connection with the idea, which I have presented of the early sentiment of community independence, I will add the very striking fact that one of the colonies, about the time that they had resolved to unite for the purpose of achieving their independence, addressed the colonial congress to know in what condition they would be in the interval between their separation from the government of Great Britain and the establishment of the government for the colonies. The answer of the colonial congress was exactly that which might have been expected--exactly that which state rights democracy would answer to-day, to such an inquiry--that they must take care of their domestic polity, that the congress "had nothing to do with it." [Applause.] If such sentiment continued--if it governed in every state--if representatives were chosen upon it--then your halls of legislation would not be disturbed about the question of the domestic concerns of the different states. The peace of the country would not be hazarded by the arraignment of the family relations of people over whom the government has no control. In harmony working together, in co-intelligence for the conservation of the interests of the country, in protection to the states and the development of the great ends for which the government was established, what effects might not be produced? As our government increased in expansion, it would increase in its beneficent influence upon the people; we should increase in fraternity; and it would be no longer a wonder to see a man coming from a southern state to address a Democratic audience in Boston. [Applause, cries of "good, good."]

But I have referred to the fact that, at an early period, Massachusetts stood pre-eminently forward among those who asserted community independence. And this reminds me of an incident, in illustration, which occurred when President Washington visited Boston, and John Hancock was Governor. The latter is reported to have declined to call upon the President, because he contended that every man who came within the limits of Massachusetts must yield rank and precedence to the Governor of the State; and only surrendered the point on account of his personal regard and respect for the character of George Washington. I honor him for it,--value it as one of the early testimonies in favor of State Rights, and wish all our governors had the same high estimate of the dignity of the office of Governor of a State as had that great and glorious man. [Applause.]

Thus it appears that the founders of this government were the true Democratic States Rights men. That Democracy was States rights, and States rights was Democracy, and it is to-day. Your resolutions breathe it. The Declaration of Independence embodies the sentiment which had lived in the hearts of the people for many years before its formal assertion. Our fathers asserted that great principle--the right of the people to choose the government for themselves--that government rested upon the consent of the governed. In every form of expression it uttered the same idea, community independence, and the dependence of the government upon the community over which it existed. It was an American principle, the great spirit which animated our country then, and it were well if more inspired us now. But I have said that this State sovereignty--this community independence--has never been surrendered, and that there is no power in the federal government to coerce a State. Does any one ask, then, how it is that a State is to be held to its obligations? My answer is: by its honor, and the obligation is the more sacred to observe every feature of the compact, because there is no power to force obedience. The great error of the confederation was that it attempted to act upon the States. It was found impracticable, and our present form of government was adopted, which acts upon individuals and does not attempt to act upon States.

The question was considered in the convention which framed the constitution, and after discussion the proposition to give power to the general government to enforce upon a resistant State obedience to the law was rejected. It was upon this ground of exemption from compulsion that the compact of the States became a sacred obligation; and it was upon this honorable fulfilment principally that our fathers depended for the security of the rights which the Constitution was designed to secure. [Applause.]

The fugitive slave compact in the Constitution of the United States implied that the States should fulfil it voluntarily. They expected the States to legislate so as to secure the rendition of fugitives.

And in 1788 it was a matter of complaint that the colony of Florida did not restore fugitive negroes from the United States who escaped into that colony, and a committee, composed of Hamilton, of New York, Sedgwick, of Massachusetts, and Madison, of Virginia, reported resolutions in the Congress instructing the committee for foreign affairs to address the charge d'affaires at Madrid to apply to his majesty of Spain to issue orders to his governor to compel them to secure the rendition of fugitive negroes to any one who should go there entitled to receive them. This was the sentiment of the committee, and they added, by way of example, as the States would return any slaves from Florida who might escape into their limits.

When the Constitutional requirement was imposed, who could have doubted that every State faithful to its obligations would comply without raising questions as to whether the institution should or should not exist in another community over which they had no control. Congress was at last forced by the failures of the States, to legislate on the subject, and this has been one of the causes by which you have been disturbed. You have been called upon to make war against a law which would never have been enacted, if each State had faithfully discharged the obligation imposed by the compact of the Constitution. [Cheers.]

There is another question connected with this negro agitation. It is in relation to the right to hold slaves in the Territories. What power has Congress to declare what shall be property? None, in the territory or elsewhere. Have the States by separate legislation the power to prescribe the condition upon which a citizen may enter on and enjoy the common property of the United States? Clearly not. Shall those who first go into the territory, deprive any citizen of the United States subsequently emigrating thither, of those rights which belong to him as an equal owner of the soil? Certainly not. Sovereignty jurisdiction can only pass to these inhabitants when the States, the owners of that territory, shall recognize the inhabitants as an independent community, and admit it to become an equal State of the Union. Until then the Constitution and laws of the United States must be the rules governing within the limits of a territory. The Constitution recognizes all property gives equal privileges to every citizen of the States; and it would be a violation of its fundamental principles to attempt any discrimination. [Applause.] Viewed in any of its phases, political, moral, social, general, or local, what is there to sustain this agitation in relation to other people's negroes, unless it be a bridge over which to pass into office--a ready capital in politics available to missionaries staving at home-reformers of things which they do not go to learn--preachers without and audience--overseers without laborers and without wages--war-horses who snuff the battle afar off, and cry: " Aha! aha! I am afar off from the battle." [Great laughter and applause.]

Thus it is that the peace of the Union is destroyed; thus it is that brother is arrayed against brother; thus it is that the people come to consider--not how they can promote each other's interests, but how they may successfully war upon them. And the political agitator like the vampire fans the victim to which he clings but to destroy.

Among culprits there is none more odious to my mind than a public officer who takes an oath to support the Constitution--the compact between the States binding each for the common defence and general welfare of the other--yet retains to himself a mental reservation that he will war upon the principles he has sworn to maintain, and upon the property rights the protection of which are part of the compact of the Union. [Applause.]

It is a crime too low to be named before this assembly: It is one which no man with self-respect would ever commit. To swear that he will support the Constitution--to take an office which belongs in many of its relations to all the States; and to use it as a means of injuring a portion of the States of whom he is thus the representative; is treason to every thing honorable in man. It is the base and cowardly attack of him who gains the confidence of another, in order that he may wound him. [Applause.]

But we have heard it argued--have seen it published--a petition has been circulated for signers, announcing that there was an incompatibility between the sections; that the Union had been tried long enough, and that it had proved to be necessary to separate from those sections of the Union in which the curse of slavery existed. Ah! those modern saints, so much wiser than our fathers, have discovered an incompatibility requiring separation in those relations which existed when the Union was formed. They have found the remnants only of a diversity which existed when South Carolina sent her rice to Boston, and Maryland and Pennsylvania and New York brought in their funds for her relief.

They have found the remnants only; for from that day to this the difference between the people has been constantly decreasing, and the necessity for union which then arose in no small degree from the diversity of product, and soil and climate, has gone on increasing, both by the extension of our own territory and the introduction of new tropical products; so that whilst the difference between the people has diminished, the diversity in the products has increased, and that motive for union which your fathers found exists in a higher degree than it did when they resolved to be united.

Diversity there is of occupation, of habits, of education, of character. But it is not of that extreme kind which proves incompatibility, or even incongruity; for your Massachusetts man, when he comes to Mississippi, adopts our opinions and our institutions, and frequently becomes the most extreme southern man among us. [Great applause.] As our country has extended--as new products have been introduced into it, the free trade which blesses our Union, has been of increasing value.

And it is not an unfortunate circumstance that this diversity of pursuit and character has survived the condition which produced it. Originally it sprang in no small degree from natural causes. Massachusetts became a manufacturing and a commercial State because of the connection between her fine harbor and water power, resulting from the fact that the streams make their last leap into the sea, so that the ship of commerce brought the staple to the manufacturing power. This made you a commercial and manufacturing people. In the Southern States great plains interpose between the last leaps of the streams and the sea. Those plains most proximate to navigation, were the first cultivated, and the sea bore their products to the most approachable water power, there to be manufactured. This was the first cause of the difference. Then your longer and more severe winters--your soil not as favorable for agriculture, also contributed to make you a manufacturing and commercial people.

After the controlling cause had passed away--after railroads had been built--after the steam engine had become a motive power for a large part of machinery, the characteristics originally stamped by natural causes continued the diversity of pursuit. Is it fortunate or otherwise? I say it is fortunate. Your interest is to remain a manufacturing and ours to remain an agricultural people.

Your prosperity is to receive our staple and to manufacture it, and ours to sell it to you and buy the manufactured goods. [Applause.] This is an interweaving of interests, which makes us all the richer and all the happier.

But this accursed agitation, this offensive, injurious intermeddling with the affairs of other people, and this alone it is that will promote a desire in the mind of any one to separate these great and growing States. [Applause.]

The seeds of dissension may be sown by invidious reflections. Men may be goaded by the constant attempt to infringe upon rights and to traduce community character, and in the resentment which follows it is not possible to tell how far the case may be driven. I therefore plead to you now to arrest a fanaticism which has been evil in the beginning, and must be evil to the end. You may not have the numerical power requisite; and those at a distance may not understand how many of you there are desirous to put a stop to the course of this agitation. But let your language and your acts teach them to appreciate a faithful self-denying minority. I have learned since I have been in New England the vast mass of true State Rights Democrats to be found within its limits--though not represented in the halls of Congress.

And if it comes to the worst; if, availing themselves of a majority in the two Houses of Congress, our opponents should attempt to trample upon the Constitution; to violate the rights of the States; to infringe upon our equality in the Union, I believe that even in Massachusetts, though it has not had a representative in Congress for many a day, the State Rights Democracy, in whose breasts beats the spirit of the revolution, can and will whip the Black Republicans. [Great applause.] I trust we shall never be thus purified, as it were, by fire; but that the peaceful progressive revolution of the ballot box will answer all the glorious purposes of the Constitutional Union. [Applause.]

I marked that the distinguished orator and statesman who preceded me in addressing you used the words national and constitutional in such relations to each other as to show that in his mind the one was a synonym of the other. And does he not do so with reason? We became a nation by the constitution; whatever is national springs from the constitution; and national and constitutional are convertible terms. [Applause.]

Your candidate for the high office of governor--whom I have been once or twice on the point of calling your governor, and whom I hope I may be able soon to call so, [applause]--in his remarks to you has presented the same idea in another form. And well may Massachusetts orators, without even perceiving what they are saying, utter sentiments which lie at the foundation of your colonial as well as your revolutionary history, which existed in Massachusetts before the revolution, and have existed since, whenever the true spirit which comes down from the revolutionary sires has been aroused into utterance within her limits. [Applause.]

It has been not only, my friends, in this increasing and mutual dependence of interest that we have formed new bonds. Those bonds are both material and mental. Every improvement in the navigation of a river, every construction of a railroad, has added another link to the chain which encircles us, another facility for interchange and new achievements, whether it has been in arts or in science, in war or in manufactures, in commerce or agriculture, success, unexampled success has constituted for us a common and proud memory, and has offered to us new sentiments of nationality.

Why, then, I would ask, do we see these lengthened shadows, which follow in the course of our political day? is it because the sun is declining to the horizon? Are they the shadows of evening; or are they, as I hopefully believe, but the mists which are exhaled by the sun as it rises, but which are to be dispersed by its meridian splendor? Are they but evanescent clouds that flit across but cannot obscure the great purposes for which the Constitution was established?

I hopefully look forward to the reaction which will establish the fact that our sun is yet in the ascendant--that the cloud which has covered our political prospect is but a mist of the morning--

that we are again to be amicably divided in opinion upon measures of expediency, upon questions of relative interest, upon discussions as to the rights of the States, and the powers of the federal government,--such discussion as is commemorated in this historical picture [pointing to the painting.] There your own great Statesman, Webster, addresses his argument to our brightest luminary, the incorruptible Calhoun, who leans over to catch the accents of eloquence that fall from his lips. [Loud applause.]

They differed as Statesmen and philosophers; they railed not, warred not against each other; they stood to each other in the relation of affection and regard. And never did I see Mr. Webster so agitated, never did I hear his voice so falter, as when he delivered his eulogy on John C. Calhoun. [Applause.]

But allusion was made to my own connection with your favorite departed Statesman. I will only say on this occasion, that very early in the commencement of my congressional life, Mr. Webster was arraigned for an offence which affected him most deeply. He was no accountant; all knew that there was but little of mercantile exactness in his habits. He was arraigned on a pecuniary charge--the misapplication of what is known as the secret service fund; and I was one of the committee that had to investigate the charge. I endeavored to do justice, to examine the evidence with a view to ascertain the truth. As an American I hoped he would come out without stain or smoke upon his garments. But however the fame of so distinguished an American Statesman might claim such hopes, the duty was rigidly to inquire, and rigorously to do justice. The result was that he was acquitted of every charge that was made against him, and it was equally my pride and my pleasure to vindicate him in every form which lay within my power. [Applause.] No man who knew Daniel Webster, would have expected less of him. Had our position been reversed, none such could have believed that he would with a view to a judgment ask whether a charge was made against a Massachusetts man or a Mississippian. No! it belonged to a lower, a later, and I trust a shorter lived race of statesmen ["hear," "hear,"] to measure all facts by considerations of latitude and longitude. [Warm applause.]

I honor that sentiment which makes us oftentimes too confident, and to despise too much the danger of that agitation which disturbs the peace of the country. I honor that feeling which believes the Constitutional Union too strong to be shaken. But at the same time I say, in sober judgment, it will not do to treat too lightly the danger which has beset and which still impends over us. Who has not heard our Constitutional Union compared to the granite cliffs which line the sea and dash back the foam of the waves, unmoved by their fury. Recently I have stood upon New England's shore, and have seen the waves of a troubled sea dash upon the granite which frowns over the ocean, have seen the spray thrown back from the cliff, and the receding wave fret like the impotent rage of baffled malice. But when the tide had ebbed, I saw that the rock was seamed and worn by the ceaseless beating of the sea, and fragments riven from the rock were lying on the beach.

Thus the waves of sectional agitation are dashing themselves against the granite patriotism of the land. If long continued, that too must show the seams and scars of the conflict. Sectional hostility must sooner or later produce political fragments. The danger lies at your door, it is time to arrest it. It is time that men should go back to the origin of our institutions. They should drink the waters of the fountain, ascend to the source, of our colonial history.

You, men of Boston, go to the street where the massacre occurred in 1770. There learn how your fathers unfaltering stood for community right. And near the same spot mark how proudly the delegation of the democracy came to demand the removal of the troops from Boston, and how the venerable Samuel Adams stood asserting the rights of the people, dauntless as Hampden, clear and eloquent as Sidney.

All over our country these monuments, instructive to the present generation, of what our fathers felt and said and did, are to be found. In the library of your association for the collection of your early history, I found a letter descriptive of the reading of the address to his army by Gen. Washington during one of those winters when he sought shelter for the ill clad, unshod, but victorious army with which he achieved the independence we enjoy; he had built a log cabin for a meeting house, and there reading his address, his sight failed him, he put on his glasses and with emotion which manifested the reality of his feelings, said, "I have grown gray in the service of my country, and now I am growing blind." Who can measure the value of such incidents in a people's history? It is a privilege to have access to documents, which cause us to realize the trials, the patient endurance, the hardy virtue and moral grandeur of the men from whom we inherit our political institutions, and to whose teachings it were well that the present generations should constantly refer.

If you choose still further to stretch your vision to South Carolina, you will find a parallel to that devotion to their country's cause which illustrates the early history of the Democrats of Boston. The prisoners at Charleston, when confined upon the hulks where they were exposed to the small pox, and, wasted by the progress of the infection, were brought upon the shore and assured that if they would enlist in his majesty's service they should be relieved from their present and prospective suffering, but if they refused the rations would be taken from their families, and themselves sent to the hulks and exposed to the infection. Emaciated as they were, distressed with the prospect of their families being turned into the street to starve, the spirit of independence, the devotion to liberty, was so warm within their breasts that they gave one loud hurrah for General Washington, and chose death rather than dishonor. [Loud applause.] And if from these glorious recollections, from the emotions they excite, your eye is directed to your present condition, and you mark the prosperity, the growth and honorable career of your country, I envy not the heart of that man whose pulse does not beat quicker, who does not feel within him the exultation of pride at the past glory and the future prospects of his country. These prospects are to be realized if we are only wise and true to the obligations of the compact of our fathers. For all which can sow dissension can stop the progress of the American people, can endanger the achievement of the high prospects we have before us is that miserable spirit, which, disregarding duty and honor, makes war upon the Constitution. Madness must rule the hour when American citizens, trampling as well upon the great principles at the foundation of the Declaration of Independence and the Constitution of the United States, as upon the honorable obligations which their fathers imposed upon them, shall turn with internicine hand to sacrifice themselves as well as their brethren, upon the altar of sectional fanaticism.

With these views, it will not be surprising to those who differ from me, that I feel an ardent desire for the success of the State Rights Democracy, that convinced of the destructive consequences of the heresies of their opponents, and of the evils upon which they would precipitate the country, I do not forbear to advocate, here and elsewhere, the success of that party which alone is national, on which alone I rely for the preservation of the Constitution, to perpetuate the Union, and to fulfil the purposes which it was ordained to establish and secure. [Loud cheers.]

My friends, my brethren, my countrymen--[applause]--I thank you for the patient attention you have given me. It is the first time it has been my fortune to address an audience here. It will probably be the last. Residing in a remote section of the country, with private as well as public duties to occupy the whole of my time, it would only be under some such necessity for a restoration of health as has brought me here this season, that I could ever expect to make more than a very hurried visit to any other portion of the Union than that of which I am a citizen.

I will say, then, on this occasion, that I am glad, truly glad, that it has been my fortune to stay long enough among the New Englanders to obtain a better acquaintance than one can who passes in the ordinary way through the country, at the speed of the railroad tourist. I have stayed long enough to feel that generous hospitality which evinces itself to-night, which has showed itself in every town and village of New England where I have gone--long enough to learn that though not represented in Congress, there is within the limits of New England a large mass of as true Democrats as are to be found in any portion of the Union. Their purposes, their construction of the Constitution, their hopes for the future, their respect for the past, is the same as that which exists among my beloved brethren in Mississippi. [Applause.]

It is not a great while since one who was endeavoring to pursue me with unfriendly criticism opened an article with my name and "gone to Boston!"--He seemed to think it a damaging reflection to say of me that I had gone to Boston--I wish he could have been here to look upon these Democratic faces to-night, and to listen to your resolutions and the words of your Massachusetts speakers, he might have been taught that a man might go and stay at Boston and learn better Democracy than many have acquired in other places.

I shall gratefully carry with me the recollections of this and of other meetings witnessed since I have been among you. In the hour of apprehension I will hopefully turn back to my observations here--here in this consecrated hall, where men so early devoted themselves to liberty and community independence; and will endeavor to impress upon others who know you only as you are misrepresented in the two Houses of Congress, [applause,] how true and how many are the hearts that beat for constitutional liberty, and with high resolve to respect every clause and guaranty which the Constitution contains, are pledged to faithfully uphold the rights of any and every portion of the States, and of the people. [Tremendous cheering.]

SPEECH IN THE CITY OF NEW YORK

Palace Garden Meeting, Oct. 19, 1858

COUNTRYMEN, Democrats:--When I accepted this evening the invitation to meet you here, it was to see and to hear, not to speak. I have listened with pleasure to the language addressed to you by your candidate for the highest office in the State. It is the language of patriotism; it is an appeal to the common sense of the people in favor of that fraternity on which our Union was founded, and on which alone it can long continue to exist. I have rejoiced to hear the applause with which such sentiments, when he uttered them, have been received by those here convened, and trust it is but an indication of that onward progress of reaction which I believe has already commenced, and which is to sink to the lowest depths of forgetfulness the struggle which has so long agitated the country, and prompted an internecine war against your countrymen. [Applause.]

Truly has the distinguished gentleman pointed out to you the extreme absurdity of attempting to excite you upon the ground of southern aggression upon the north. We have nothing to aggress upon. We have not now, as he has told you, the power, though once we had, to interfere with your domestic institutions. We never had the will to do so. And if we had the power now, true to the instincts and history of our fathers, we would abstain from intermeddling in your domestic affairs. [Applause.] I have no purpose on this or any other occasion to mingle in the consideration of those questions which are local to you. I am not sufficiently learned in conchology to do it if I would, [laughter,] and I have too great a respect for community independence to do it if I could. My purpose then is, simply in answer to your call, to offer you a few reflections, such as may occur to me, as I progress, upon those questions which are common to us all, and which belong to the memories of our fathers, and are linked with the hopes of our children. [Applause.] If; then, without preparation, I do it in unvarnished phrase, if I cannot carry you along with me because of the want of that flowing diction which might catch the ear, still I ask you to hear me for my cause, for it is the cause of our country, it is the cause of democracy, it is the cause of human liberty. [Applause.]

Who now stand arrayed against the democratic party? The relations of parties and the issues upon which we have been divided have changed. What now is the basis of opposition to the democratic party? It is twofold--interference with the negroes of other people, and interference with the rights now secured to foreigners who expatriate themselves and come to our land. ["Hear, hear," and applause.] To each community belongs the right to decide for itself what institutions it will have. To each people sovereign within their own sphere, belongs, and to them only belongs, the right to decide what shall be property. You have decided it for yourselves. Who shall gainsay your decision? Mississippi has decided it for herself; who has the right to gainsay her decision? The power of each people to rule over their domestic affairs lies at the foundation of that Declaration of Independence to which you owe your existence among the nations of the earth; that declaration which led your fathers into and through the war of the revolution. It is that which constitutes to-day the doctrine of State-rights, upon which it is my pride and pleasure to stand. [Applause.] Congress has no power to determine what shall be property anywhere. Congress has only such grants as are contained in the Constitution. And the Constitution confers upon it no power to rule with despotic hand over the inhabitants of the Territories. Within the limits of those Territories, the common property of the Union, you and I are equal; we are joint owners. Each of us has the right to go into those Territories, with whatever property is recognized by the Constitution of the United States. [Applause.] Congress has no power to limit or abridge that right. But the inhabitants of a Territory when as a people they come to form a State government, when they possess the power and jurisdiction which belongs to the people of New York, or any other State, have the right to decide that question, and no power upon earth has the right to decide it before that time. [Applause.]

[At this point the Young Men's Democratic National Club, with banners and transparencies, entered the garden, and were received with enthusiastic cheers.]

The dull remarks, my friends, which I was in the course of making to you, have been interrupted by a beautiful episode, which I am sure will more than exceed the whole value of the poem, if I may thus characterize my dull speech. And I am glad that foremost among all the transparencies and banners, comes this flag which speaks of the "Young Men's Democratic National Club."--[Three cheers for Davis.] It is on the young men we must rely. I have found that in every severe political struggle, where the contest on the one side was for principle, and on the other for spoils, it has been the gray-haired father and the boy with the peach bloom upon his cheek upon whom principles had to rely for support. My own generation--and I regret to say it--seems too deeply steeped in the trickery of politics to be able to rise above the influence of personal and political gain into the pure field of patriotism. And I am therefore glad to see the "Young Men's Democratic National Club" leading this procession.

But to return to the argument I was making. I said that Congress had no power to legislate upon what should be property anywhere; that Congress had no power to discriminate between the citizens of the different States who should go into the Territories, the common property of all the States, but that those Territories of right remained open to every citizen, and every species of property recognized in the Constitution, until the inhabitants should become a people, form a fundamental law for themselves, and, as authorized by the Constitution, assume the powers, duties, and obligations of a State. And now, my friends, I would ask you, further, of what value would a congressional decision upon that subject be? If it be a constitutional right, as I contend it is, then it is a matter for judicial decision. If Congress should assert that such is not the right of each of our citizens, and the courts appointed as an arbiter in such cases should decide that it is their right, the enactment would, therefore, be void. It, on the other hand, it is not a right, but Congress should assert it to be one, and the courts should declare that no such right exists under the Constitution, then, Congress has no power to create it; and it is in this sense that Congress has not the power to establish or prohibit slavery anywhere. [Applause.]

What, then, has been the foundation of all this controversy? Your candidate has justly pointed out to you that unpatriotic struggle for sectional aggrandizement which has brought about this contest--a contest, as it were, between two contending powers for national predominance--a contest upon the one side to enlarge the majority it now possesses, and a contest upon the other side to recover the power it has lost, and become the majority. This is the attitude of hostile nations, and not of States bound together in fraternal unity. This is the feeling that one by one is cutting the strands which originally held the States together. You have seen your churches divided; you have seen trade turned aside from its accustomed channel; you have seen jealousy and uncharitableness and bickering springing up and growing stronger day by day, until at last, if it continue, the cord of union between the States reduced simply to the political strand, may not suffice to hold them together. Once united by every tie of fraternal feeling, shoulder to shoulder, step by step, our fathers went through the revolution, prompted by a common desire for the common good, and animated by devotion to the principle of popular liberty. They struggled against the mother country, because that country endeavored to legislate for the colonies, and the colonies claimed as a right that they must not be taxed except by their own representatives, and refused to submit to unconstitutional legislation. If now, in this struggle for the ascendency in power, one action should gain such predominance as would enable it, by modifying the Constitution and usurping new power, to legislate for the other, the exercise of that power would throw us back into the condition of the colonies. And if in the veins of the sons flows the blood of their sires, they would not fail to redeem themselves from tyranny even should they be driven to resort to revolution. [Applause.]

And what is the other question of difference now? It is the agitation, as a national question, of the right of foreigners to suffrage within these States. Now, I ask, what power has Congress over the question? Yet members to Congress are elected upon that question. How would Congress legislate upon it?--They say, by modifying the naturalization laws. What do those laws confer? The right to hold real estate and the right to devise it by will; the right to sue and be sued in the courts of the United States; and the rights to receive passports and protection from the government of the United States. Who wishes to withhold those privileges from foreigners? Nobody alleges it. But they say that the ballot-box must be protected from foreign votes. Has Congress the right to say that foreigners shall not vote within the limits of your State? Are you willing to leave that to Congress? [Cries of " No, no, no," and applause.] In some of the States, by State legislation, foreigners are permitted to vote before they can become citizens under the naturalization laws. The naturalization laws are not, therefore, controlling over the question of suffrage. The power of Congress is limited to the establishment of a uniform rule of naturalization throughout the States. But what further do they couple with these demands which they make for congressional legislation? They proclaim their purpose to be to exclude paupers and criminals from abroad.--Do paupers and criminals come for the right of suffrage? They come here for bread, or to fly from the laws which they have violated. Whether they shall be entitled to vote or not, would neither increase nor diminish the number of that class by a single individual. But, my friends, who is a pauper, or who is a criminal? Is a man a pauper merely because he comes here without property, without money in his purse? Go, look along your lines of internal improvements, where every mile has mingled with it the bones of some foreigner who labored to create it. Go to your battle fields, where your flag has been borne triumphantly, and where fresh laurels have been added to the brow of your country, and there you will find the sod dyed as deep by the blood of the foreign born as by that of the native citizen. [Applause.] Is the able-bodied man, who comes here to contribute to your national interests by building up your public works, or aiding in the erection of your architectural constructions, or who bears your flag in the hour of danger, and who bleeds and dies for your country, is he the pauper you desire to exclude? And who is the criminal? Is it he who, flying from the persecution of despotic governments, seeks our land as the Huguenot did, as did Soule, the stern American orator, as many others within your limits have done under more recent struggles for liberty in Europe? [Applause.] Then, who are the paupers and criminals? Is that to be decided by the ruling of other countries, by the laws of France, or of England? Or is it to be decided by your own laws, by your own rules of judicature? If by the latter, then there is no good ground for controversy. We do not advocate that any country shall empty its poor houses, get rid of the duty of supporting its paupers, and throw that charge upon us. We could not permit any country to empty its prisons and penitentiaries to mingle that portion of its population with ours. But we do war against the use of terms that delude the people, and are intended to exclude the high-spirited and hard-working men who contribute to the bone, the sinew, and the wealth of our country. [Applause.]

Such, then, my friends, is the opposition to the democracy, the only national party. The opposition, I say, claims two things from the federal government, neither of which it has the constitutional power to perform. It agitates this section of the Union in relation to property which it has not, and of which, I say, it knows literally nothing. For had the orator (Mr. Giddings) who was quoted to-night, known anything of the relations between the master and the slave, he would not have talked of the slave armed with the British bayonet. Our doors are unlocked at night; we live among them with no more fear of them than of our cows and oxen. We lie down to sleep trusting to them for our defence, and the bond between the master and the slave is as near as that which exists between capital and labor anywhere. Now, about the idea of British bayonets in the hands of slaves: The delusion which has always excited my surprise the most has been that which has led so many of the northern men to strike hands with the British abolitionists to make war on their southern brethren. If they could effect their ends, and Great Britain could insert the wedge which should separate the States, what further use would she have for the northern section? You are the competitors of Great Britain in the vast field of manufacture, whom she most fears, and though she may be with you in the scheme which would effect a separation of these States, yet the moment that separation should be effected she would be under the promptings of interest your worst enemy. [Applause.] Our fathers fought and bled to secure the common interests of the country. They reclaimed us from colonial bondage to national independence. They stamped upon it free trade in order that the interests of all might be promoted, that each section might be interwoven with the other--in order that there might be the strongest bond of mutual dependence. And step by step, from that day to this, that common and mutual dependence has been growing.

From the seeds of narrow sectionality and purblind fanaticism, have sprung the tares which threaten the principles of that declaration which made the Colonies independent States, and of that compact by which the States were united by a bond to-day far more valuable than when it was signed. You have among you politicians of a philosophic turn, who preach a high morality; a system of which they are the discoverers, and it is to be hoped will long remain the exclusive possessors. They say, it is true the Constitution dictates this, the Bible inculcates that; but there is a higher law than those, and call upon you to obey that higher law, of which they are the inspired givers. [Laughter and applause.] Men who are traitors to the compact of their fathers--men who have perjured the oaths they have themselves taken--they who wish to steep their hands in the blood of their brothers; these are the moral law-givers who proclaim a higher law than the Bible, the Constitution, and the laws of the land. This higher-law doctrine, it strikes me, is the most convenient one I ever heard of for the criminal. You, no doubt, have a law which punishes a man for stealing a horse or a bale of goods. But the thief would find more convenient a higher law which would justify him in keeping the stolen goods. The doctrine is now advanced to you only in its relation to property of the Southern States, thus it is the pill gilded, to conceal its bitterness; but it will re-act deeply upon yourselves if you accept it. What security have you for your own safety if every man of vile temper, of low instincts, of base purpose, can find in his own heart a higher law than that which is the rule of society, the Constitution, and the Bible? These higher-law preachers should be tarred and feathered, and whipped by those they have thus instigated. This, my friends, is what was called in good old revolutionary times. Lynch Law. It is sometimes the very best law, because it deals summary justice upon those who would otherwise escape from all other kinds of punishment. The man who with sycophantic face and studied phrase, and with assumed philosophic morality, preaches treason to the Constitution and the dictates of all human society, is a fit object for a Lynch law that would be higher than any he could urge. [Applause.]

My democratic friends, I am deeply gratified by the exhibition which is before me. I see here a field of faces, assembled in the name of Democracy, and over it high, bright and multiplied for the occasion, as stars have been added by Democracy to the flag of our country, blaze the lights which typify democratic principles, pointing upward, to guide our country to that haven of prosperity which our fathers saw in the distant future, and which they left it for their sons to attain. It we are true to ourselves, true to the obligations which the Constitution imposes upon us, and if we are wise and energetic in the struggles which lie before us, our path is onward to more of national greatness than ever people before possessed. We are held together by that two-fold government, which is susceptible of being made perfect in the small spheres of State limits, and capable of the greatest imperial power, by the combination of these municipal powers into one for foreign action. It is a form of government such as the wit of man never devised until our fathers, with a wisdom that approached inspiration, framed the Constitution, and transmitted it as a legacy to us. It devolves upon every one of you, to see that each provision of that Constitution is cordially and faithfully observed. If cordially and faithfully observed, the powers of hell and of earth combined can never shake the happiness and prosperity of the people of the United States. [Applause.] With every revolving year there will arise new motives for holding tenaciously to each other. With every revolving cycle there will come new sources of pride and national sentiment to the people. Year after your flag will grow more brilliant, by the addition of fresh stars, recording the growth of our political family, and onward, over land and over sea, the progress of American principles, of human liberty illustrated, and protected by the power of the United States, will hold its way to a triumph such as the earth has never witnessed. [Applause.] On the other hand, what do we see? A picture so black that if I could unveil it, I would not in this cheery moment expose a scene so chilling to your enthusiasm, and revolting to your patriotic hearts. My friends, feeling that I have already detained you too long, I now return to you my cordial thanks for the kindness with which you have received me to-night.

SPEECH BEFORE THE MISSISSIPPI LEGISLATURE

MISSISSIPPIANS: Again it is my privilege and good fortune to be among you, to stand before those whom I have loved, for whom I have labored, by whom I have been trusted and honored, and here to answer for myself. Time and disease have frosted my hair, impaired my physical energies, and furrowed my brow, but my heart remains unchanged, and its every pulsation is as quick, as strong, and as true to your interests, your honor, and fair fame, as in the period of my earlier years.

It is known to many of you, that at the close of the last session of Congress, wasted by protracted, violent disease, I went, in accordance with medical advice, to the Northeastern coast of the United States. Against the opinion of my physician, I had remained at Washington until my public duties were closed, and then adopted the only course which it was believed gave reasonable hope for a final restoration to health--that is, sought a region where I should be exempt from the heat of summer, and from political excitement.

In one respect at least, this accorded with my own feelings, for physically and mentally depressed, fearful that I should never again be able to perform my part in the trials to which Mississippi might be subjected, I turned away from my fellows with such feelings as the wounded elk leaves his herd, and seeks the covert, to die alone. Misrepresentation and calumny followed me even to the brink of the grave, and with hyena instinct would have pursued me beyond it.

The political positions which I had always occupied, justified the expectation that in New England I should be left in loneliness. In this I was disappointed; courtesy and kindness met me on my first landing, and attended me to the time of my departure. The manifestations of comity and hospitality, given by the generous and the noble, aroused the petty hostility of the more extreme of the Black Republicans, and their newspapers assailed me with the low abuse which for years I had been accustomed to receive at their hands. I had always despised their malice and defied their enmity; their assaults did not surprise me, but when I found them echoed in Southern papers, it did astonish, I will confess, it did pain me, not for any injury apprehended to myself, but for its evil effect upon the cause with which I was identified.

Was it expected that to public and private manifestations of kindness by the people of Maine, I should return denunciation and repel their generous approaches with epithets of abuse? If they had deserved such reproach, they could not merit it at my hands. A guest hospitably attended, it would have been inconsistent with the character of a gentleman, to have done less than acknowledge their kindness, and it was not in my nature to feel otherwise than grateful to them for the many manifestations of a desire to render pleasant and beneficial the sojourn of an invalid among them. But they did not deserve it, and I am happy to state as the result of my acquaintance with them, that we have a large body of true friends among them, men who maintain our constitutional rights as explicitly and as broadly as we assert them, and who have performed this service with the foreknowledge that they were thereby to sacrifice their political prospects, at least, until through years of patient exertion they should correct error, suppress fanaticism, and build for themselves a structure on the basis of truth, which had long been unwelcome and might not soon be understood.

But there were other evidences of regard more valuable to me than exhibitions of personal kindness. Regard for the people of Mississippi, founded on a special attention to their history; the gallant services of your sons in the field, were publicly claimed as property which Mississippi could not appropriate to herself; but which were part of the common wealth of the nation, and belonged equally to the people of Maine. Could I be insensible to such recognition of the honorable fame of Mississippi? No, the memory of the gallant dead, who died at Monterey and Buena Vista, forbade it.

At a subsequent period, when in Massachusetts, one of her distinguished sons, (Gen. Cushing,) paid a compliment to the feat performed by the Mississippi Regiment in checking the enemies cavalry on the field of Buena Vista one Black Republican newspaper denied the originality of the movement, and claimed it to have been previously performed by an English regiment at Quatre Bras. This claim was unfounded; the service performed by the British Regiment having been of a totally different character and for a different purpose.--A Southern paper, however, has gone one step beyond that of the Massachusetts paper, and denies the merit claimed for the service rendered by saying that it was the result of accident, growing out of the peculiar conformation of the ground on which the regiment rallied and that it was necessary for the safety of the regiment, being like the act of a man who leaps from a burning ship and takes the chance of drowning.

If this only affected myself, I should leave it, like other misrepresentations, unnoticed, but it concerns the hard earned reputation of the regiment I commanded. It affects the fame of Mississippi, and propagates an error which may pollute the current of history.

We live in an age of progress, and it requires a progressive age to produce a military critic who should discover that a soldier deserved no credit for availing himself of the accidents of ground. One half of the science of war consists in teaching how to take advantage of the irregularities of the ground on which military movements are to be made, or defensive works are to be constructed. The highest reputation of Generals in every age has resulted in their skill in military topography. The most marked compliment ever paid by one General to another, was that of Napoleon to Cæsar, when he halted on his encampments without a previous reconnoisance. But the regiment did not rally as stated, for it had not been dispersed; neither was their movement the result of their own necessity, or adopted for their own safety. They were marching by the flank, on the side of a ravine, when the enemy's cavalry were seen approaching. They could have halted on the side of the ravine, which was so precipitous that they would have been there as sate from a charge as if they had been in Mississippi. They could have gone down into the ravine, and have been concealed even from the sight of the cavalry. The necessity was to prevent the cavalry from passing to the rear of our line of battle, where they might have attacked, and probably carried our batteries, which were then without the protection of our infantry escort. It was our country's necessity and not our own which prompted the service there performed. For this the regiment was formed square across the plain, and there stood motionless as a rock, silent as death, and eager as a greyhound for the approach of the enemy, at least nine times, numerically, their superiors. Some Indiana troops were formed on the brink of the ravine with the right flank of the Mississippi Regiment, constituting one branch of what has been called the "V". When the enemy had approached as near as he dared and seemed to shrink from contact with the motionless, resolute living wall which stood before him, the angry crack of the Mississippi rifle was heard, and as the smoke rose and the dust fell, there remained of the host which so lately stood before us but the fallen and the flying. The rear of our line of battle was again secured, and a service had been rendered which in no small degree contributed to the triumph which finally perched upon the banner of the United States.

I am not a disinterested, and may not be a competent judge, but I know how I thought, and still believe, that your sons, given by you to the public service in the war with Mexico, have not received the full measure of the credit which was their due. They, however, received so much that we might be content to rest on the history as it has been written. But it constitutes a reason why we should not permit any of the leaves to be unjustly torn away.

To return to the consideration of the less important subject, the misrepresentation of myself; I will again express the surprise I felt that when abolition papers were assailing me with a view to destroy any power which I might acquire to correct the error which had been instilled into the minds of the people of the North in relation to Southern sentiments and Southern institutions, that they should have received both aid and comfort from Southern newspapers, and been bolstered up in the attempt to misrepresent my political position. When the charge was made, which was copied in Northern papers, that I had abandoned those with whom I co-operated in 1852, to produce a separation of the States, my friend, the editor of the Mississippian, seeing the misrepresentation of my position, and naturally supposing, as we had no discussion in 1852, the reference must have been made to the canvass of 1851, quoted from the resolutions of the State-Rights Democratic Convention, and from an address published by myself to the people, to show that my position was the reverse of that assigned to me. Before proceeding, I will advert to a reference which has been made to him, as my "organ." He is no more my "organ" than I am his. We have generally concurred, I and have been able to understand and anticipate his positions as he has mine. I am indebted to him for many favors. He is indebted to me for nothing. As Democrats, as gentlemen, as friends, we occupy to each other the relation of exact equality.

Notwithstanding that irrefutable answer to the charge, it has been reiterated, and, as before, located in the year 1852. It is known to you all that our discussions were in 1851. I then favored a convention of the Southern States, that we might take counsel together, as to the future which was to be anticipated, from the legislation of 1850. The decision of the State was to acquiesce in the legislation of that year, with a series of resolutions in relation to future encroachments. I submitted to the decision of the people, and have in good faith adhered to the line of conduct which it imposed. Therefore in 1852 there is no record from which to disprove any allegation, but you know the charge to be utterly unfounded, and charity alone can suppose its reiteration was innocently made. Neither in that year nor in any other, have I ever advocated a dissolution of the Union, or the separation of the State of Mississippi from the Union, except as the last alternative, and have not considered the remedies which lie within that extreme as exhausted, or ever been entirely hopeless of their success. I hold now, as announced on former occasions, that whilst occupying a seat in the Senate, I am bound to maintain the Government of the Constitution, and in no manner to work for its destruction; that the obligation of the oath of office, Mississippi's honor and my own, require that, as a Senator of the United States, there should be no want of loyalty to the Constitutional Union. Whenever Mississippi shall resolve to separate from the Confederacy, I will expect her to withdraw her representatives from the General Government, to which they are accredited. If I should ever, whilst a Senator, deem it my duty to assume an attitude of hostility to the Union, I should, immediately thereupon, feel bound to resign the office, and return to my constituency to inform them of the fact. It was this view of the obligations of my position, which caused me, on various occasions, to repel, with such indignation, the accusation of being a disunionist, while holding the office of Senator of the United States.

I have been represented as having, advocated "Squatter Sovereignty" in a speech made at Bangor, in the State of Maine, A paragraph has been published purporting to be an extract from that speech, and vituperative criticism, and forced construction have exhausted themselves upon it, with deductions which are considered authorized, because they are not denied in the paragraph published.

In this case, as in that of the charge in relation to my position in 1852, there is no record with which to answer. I never made a speech at Bangor. And a fair mind would have sought for the speech to see how far the general context explained the paragraph, before indulging in hostile criticism.

Senator Douglas, in a speech at Alton, adopting the paragraph published, and evidently drawing his opinion from the unfair construction which had been put upon it, claims to quote from a speech made by me at Bangor, to sustain the position taken by him at Freeport. He says:

"You will find in a recent speech, delivered by that able and eloquent statesman, Hon. Jefferson Davis, at Bangor, Maine, that he took the same view of this subject that I did in my Freeport speech. He there said:"

"'If the inhabitants of any territory should refuse to enact such laws and police regulations as would give security to their property and his, it would be rendered more or less valueless, in proportion to the difficulty of holding it without such protection. In the case of property in the labor of a man, or what is usually called slave property, the insecurity would be so great that the owner could not ordinarily retain it. Therefore, though the right would remain, the remedy being withheld, it would follow that the owner would be practically debarred, by the circumstances of the case, from taking slave property into a Territory where the sense of the inhabitants was opposed to its introduction. So much for the oft repeated fallacy of forcing slavery upon any community.'"

It is fair to suppose, if the Senator had known where to find the speech from which this extract was taken, that he would have examined it before proceeding to make such use of it. And I can but believe, if he had taken the paragraph free from the distortion which it had undergone from others, that he must have seen it bore no similitude to his position at Freeport, and could give no countenance to the doctrine he then announced. He there said:

"The next question Mr. Lincoln propounded to me is: 'Can the people of a territory exclude slavery from their limits by any fair means, before it comes into the Union as a State?' I answer emphatically, as Mr. Lincoln has heard me answer a hundred times, on every stump in Illinois, that in my opinion, the people of a territory can, by lawful means, exclude slavery before it comes ill as a State. [Cheers.] Mr. Lincoln knew that I had given that answer over and over again. He heard me argue the Nebraska bill on that principle all over the State, in 1854, and '55, and '56, and he has now no excuse to pretend to have any doubt upon that subject. Whatever the Supreme Court may hereafter decide as on the abstract question of whether slavery may go in under the Constitution or not, the people of a territory have the lawful means to admit or exclude it as they please for the reason that slavery cannot exist a day or an hour anywhere unless supported by local police regulations, furnishing remedies aid means of enforcing the right of holding slaves. Those local aid police regulations can only be furnished by the local Legislature. If the people of the Territory are opposed to slavery they will elect members to the Legislature who will adopt unfriendly legislation to it. If they are for it, they will adopt the legislative measures friendly to slavery. Hence no matter what may be the decision of the Supreme Court, on that abstract questions still the right of the people to make it a slave territory or a free territory, is perfect and complete under the Nebraska Bill. I hope Mr. Lincoln will deem my answer satisfactory on this point." This is the distinct assertion of the power of territorial legislation to admit or exclude slavery; of the first in the race of migration who reach a territory, the common property of the people of the United States to enact laws for the exclusion of other joint owners of the territory, who may in the exercise of their equal right to enter the common property, choose to take with them property recognized by the Constitution, built not acceptable to the first emigrants to the Territory. That Senator had too often and too fully discussed with me the question of "squatter sovereignty" to be justified in thus mistaking my opinion. The difference between us is as wide as that of one who should assert the right to rob from him who admitted the power. It is true, as I stated it at that time, all property requires protection from the society in the midst of which it is held. This necessity does not confer a right to destroy, but rather creates an obligation to protect. It is true as I stated it, that slave property peculiarly requires the protection of society, and would ordinarily become valueless in the midst of a community, which would seek to seduce the slave front his master, and conceal him whilst absconding, and as jurors protect each other in any suit which the master might bring for damages. The laws of the United States, through the courts of the United States, might enable the master to recover the slave wherever he could find him. But you all know, in such a community as I have supposed, that a slave inclined to abscond would become utterly useless, and that was the extent of the admission.

The extract on which reliance has been placed was taken from a speech made at Portland, and both before and after the extract, the language employed conclusively disproves the construction, which unfriendly criticism has put upon the detached passage. Immediately preceding it, the following language was used:

"The Territory being the common property of States, equals in the Union, and bound by the Constitution which recognizes property in slaves, it is an abuse of terms to call aggression the migration into that Territory of one of its joint owners, because carrying with him any species of property recognized by the Constitution of the United States. The Federal Government has no power to declare what is property enywhere.{sic} The power of each State cannot extend beyond its own limits. As a consequence, therefore, whatever is property in any of the States, must be so considered in any of the territories of the United States until they reach to the dignity of community independence, when the subject matter will be entirely under the control of the people, and be determined by their fundamental law. If the inhabitants of any territory should refuse to enact such laws and police regulations as would give security to their property or to his, it would be rendered more or less valueless, in proportion to the difficulty of holding it without such protection. In the case of property in the labor of man, or what is usually called slave property, the insecurity would be so great that the owner could not ordinarily retain it. Therefore, though the right would remain, the remedy being withheld, it would follow that the owner would be practically debarred by the circumstances of the case, from taking slave property into a territory where the sense of the inhabitants was opposed to its introduction. So much for the oft repeated fallacy of forcing slavery upon any community."

And in a subsequent part of the same speech, the matter was treated of in this wise:

"The South had not asked Congress to extend slavery into the territories, and he in common with most other Southern statesmen, denied the existence of any power to do so. He held it to be the creed of the Democracy, both in the North and the South, that the general government had no constitutional power either to establish or prohibit slavery anywhere; a grant of power to do the one must necessarily have involved the power to do the other. Hence it is their policy not to interfere on the one side or the other, but protecting each individual in his constitutional rights, to leave every independent community to determine and adjust all domestic questions as in their wisdom may seem best."

In other speeches made elsewhere, in New England and in New York the equality of the South as joint owners was declared and maintained, as I had often done before the people of Mississippi and in the Senate of the United States when the subject was in controversy. The position taken by me in 1850, in the form of an amendment offered to one of the compromise measures of that year, was intended to assert the equal right of all property to the protection of the United States, and to deny to any legislative body the power to abridge that right. The decision of the Supreme Court in the Dred Scott case has fully sustained our position in the following passage:

"If Congress itself cannot do this, (prohibit slavery in a Territory,) if it is beyond the powers conferred on the Federal Government--it will be admitted, we presume, that it could not authorize a territorial government to exercise them. It could confer no power on any local government established by its authority, to violate the provisions of the Constitution.

"And if the Constitution recognizes the right of property of the master in a slave; and makes no distinction between that description of property and other property owned by a citizen, no tribunal, acting under the authority of the United States, whether legislative, executive, or judicial, has a right to draw such a distinction, or deny to it the benefit of the provisions and guarantees which have been provided for the protection of private property against the encroachments of the government."

At the time of the adoption of the Kansas-Nebraska bill, it certainly was understood that the constitutional rights to take slaves into any territory of the United States should thenceforth be regarded as a judicial question; and therefore special provision was made to facilitate the bringing of such questions before the Supreme Court of the United States. After the decision to which reference has just been made, the prominent advocate of the bill at the time of its enactment should have been estopped from recurring to his "squatter sovereignty" heresies, though the decision should have been different from his anticipation or desire. And as much interest has been felt in relation to his position, and some inquiry has been made as to my view of it, I will here say, that I consider him as having recanted the better opinions announced by him in 1854, and that I cannot be compelled to choose between men, one of whom asserts the power of Congress to deprive us of a constitutional right, and the other only denies the power of Congress, in order to transfer it to the territorial legislature.

Neither the one nor the other has any authority to sit in judgment on our rights under the Constitution.

Between such positions, Mississippi cannot have a preference, because she cannot recognize anything tolerable in either of them.

Having called your attention to the speech made at Portland, to show that other parts of it disprove the construction put upon the paragraph, which was taken from it, and reported to be a part of the speech delivered at Bangor, it may be as well on this occasion to state the circumstances under which the speech was made at Portland. Immediately preceding the State election, I was invited, by the democracy of that city, to address them, and my attention was especially called to a delusion practiced on the people of Maine, by which many were led to believe that there was a purpose on the part of the South, through the government of the United States, to force slavery not only into the territories, but also into the non-slaveholding States of the Union. It was represented to me that in the last Presidential canvass that one of the Senators of Maine had convinced many of the voters that if Mr. Buchanan should be elected, slavery would be forced upon Maine, and that the other Senator was arguing that the Dred Scott decision of the Supreme Court had given authority to introduce and hold slaves in that State. To counteract such impressions, injurious to the South and her friends, the remarks which have been extracted were made.

On that, as on other occasions, it was deemed a duty to correct misrepresentation and seek to vindicate our purposes from the prejudice which ignorance and agitation had created against us. If it was in my power in any degree to allay sectional excitement, to cultivate sounder opinions and a more fraternal feeling, it was a task most acceptable to me, and one for the performance of which I could not doubt your approval. But it has been my fortune to be the object of a malice which I have not striven to appease because I was conscious that it rested upon no injury or injustice inflicted by me. The land swarms with Presidential candidates, announced by their agents or their friends, or by themselves, as the mode most available for preventing too zealous and partial friends from putting them in nomination. To these it was the source of unfounded apprehension, that I went to the coast of New England, instead of returning to Mississippi. If any of them had known the necessity which kept me from home, it is fair to suppose the aspirant for such distinction could not have been guilty of the meanness of suppressing that fact, and allowing misrepresentation to do its work in my absence.

For the wretch who is doomed to go through the world bearing a personal jealousy or a personal malignity, which renders him incapable of doing justice, and studious of misrepresentation, I can only feel pity, and were it possible to feel revengeful, could consign him to no worse punishment than that of his own tormentors, the vipers nursed in his own breast.

But long have I delayed what is my chief purpose, to speak to my friends, the men whose good opinion is to me of importance only second to the approval of my own conscience. So far as they have misunderstood me, it is a pleasure to set forth the true meaning of both my words and my deeds. To my traducers I have no explanations to offer and no apologies for any one. If State Rights men in the excess of their zeal have censured me, I have no reproaches for them, but cheerfully bear the burden which may be imposed upon me by zeal in the cause to which my political life has been devoted, and in imitation of Job, would bless the State Rights Democracy of Mississippi, even if the object of its vengeance: "Though he slay me, yet will I trust in him."

If I had been asked what interpretation might possibly be put upon the published sketch of the remarks made by me at sea on the Fourth of July last, speculation would have been exhausted before it would have occurred to me that my State Rights friends would consider themselves described under the head of "trifling politicians," who could not believe that the country would remain united to repel insult to our flag as it had recently been on the occasion of the attempt to exercise visit and search in the Gulf of Mexico, under the pretext of checking the African slave trade. The publisher of that sketch has already announced that it was not a report, and that for its language I could not justly be considered responsible. To this it is needless that I should add any thing. But I have treated it, and will treat it in the view necessarily taken by those who construed it before such denial was made.

During the period of greatest adversity, in the hour of gloom and defeat, the State Rights Democracy had no cause to complain of my fealty. We struggled together, fell together, rose together, and to them I am indebted for whatever of consideration or position I possess. Endeared to me by our common suffering; grateful to them for the steadfast support with which they have honored me, accustomed to refer with pride to my identity with them, it would have been strange indeed, if when separated from them under circumstances which turned any eyes, with more than ordinary anxiety towards my home, I should then have sought an occasion to heap reproachful language upon them.

Often it has been my duty to repel the accusations of others who sought to attribute to the State Rights Democracy opinions not their own, and to impute to them the purpose to agitate for the destruction of the government we inherited. As one of the State Rights party, I deny that the language published is a picture of me or my class, and I have as little disposition now, as at any former time, to separate myself from the body of the party, with which I have so long acted, which I rejoice to see in power at home, and daily more and more respected in the other States.

I have thus defined who were not meant, and will now tell who were meant. Firsts they were the noisy agitators who were constantly disturbing the public peace and proclaiming that slavery is so great an evil, that the preservation of the Union is subordinate to the purpose of abolishing it. They who object to any protection, on the high seas or elsewhere, being given to slave property by the government of the United States; who would rejoice in any insult offered to the national flag if borne by a vessel sailing from a Southern port; and who have been for some time back circulating petitions for a dissolution of the Union on the ground of the incompatibility of the sections. And to these may be added the few, the very few of Southern men who fancying that they would have advantages out of the Union which they cannot possess within it, however fully the compact should be observed and State Equality maintained, desire its dissolution, and taking counsel of their passions, decry the labors of all who seek to preserve the government as our fathers formed it, and to develop the great purposes for which it was ordained and established.

The other phrase which has been the subject of comment was, "and this great country will remain united." How "united" is set forth in the language to which this clause was a conclusion, "united to protect our national flag whenever a foreign power, presuming on our domestic dissention, should dare to insult it." The unanimity with which men of all parties in the two houses of Congress rallied to support the executive in maintaining the rights of our flag, had been the subject of my commendation. Upon that fact the idea expressed rested. At worst it could but have evinced too much credulity, and I trust I may die believing that whenever the honor of our flag shall demand it, every mountain and valley and plain, will pour forth their hardy sons, and that shoulder to shoulder they will march against any foreign foe which shall invade the rights of any portion of the United States.

And here permit me as a duty to you, and an obligation upon myself, to pay the tribute which I believe to be due the Northern Democracy. Having formed my opinion of them upon insufficient data, I have had occasion, after much intercourse with them, to modify it. I believe that a great reaction has commenced; how far it will progress I do not pretend to say, but am hopeful that agitation will soon become unprofitable to political traders in New England, and this hope rests upon the high position taken by the Northern Democracy, and upon the increased vote which in some of the States, under the more distinct avowal of sound principles, their candidates have received. You may now often hear among them not only the unqualified defence of your constitutional rights, but the vindication of your institutions in the abstract, and in the concrete.

In the town of Portland, just preceding the election, a Democrat of large means and extensively engaged in commercial transactions and city improvements addressed the Democracy, arguing that their prosperity depended upon their connection with countries, the products of which were dependent upon slave labor; and the future growth and prosperity of their city depended upon the extension of slave labor into all countries where it could be profitably employed. He showed by a statistical statement the paralysing effect which would be produced upon their interest by the abolition of slavery. The Black Republican papers of course abused him, and compared him to Davis and Toombs, but his sound views were approved by the Democracy, and so far as I could judge, he gained consideration by their manly utterance.

A generation had been educated in error, and the South had done nothing in defence of the abstract right of slavery. Within a few years essays have been written, books have been published, by northern as well as by southern men, and with the increase of information, there has been a subsidence of prejudice, and a preparation of the mind to receive truth. Our friends are still in a minority. It would be vain to speculate as to the period when their position will be reversed. Whether sooner or later, or never, they are still entitled to our regard and respect. A few years ago those who maintained our constitutional right, and to secure it voted for the Kansas and Nebraska bill, went home to meet reproach and expulsions from public employment.

Even their social position was affected by that political act. The few years, however, which have elapsed, have produced a great change. They have recovered all except their political position. That bill which was considered when it was enacted, a Southern measure, for which Northern men bravely sacrificed their political prospects, has of late been denounced at the South as a cheat and a humbug. A poor return certainly, to those who conscientiously maintaining our rights, surrendered their popularity to secure what the men for whom they made the sacrifice now pronounce to have been a cheat. It is true that bill has recently received in some quarters a construction which its friends did not place upon it when it was enacted. But it should be judged by its terms and by contemporaneous construction.

When I visited the people of Mississippi last year, the question of greatest public excitement, was connected with the action of the Executive in relation to the admission of Kansas as a State of the Union. You had been led to suppose that the President would attempt to control the action of the convention, and if the constitution was not submitted to a popular vote, would oppose by all the means within his power, the admission of the State within the Union. You were also excited at a dogma which had been put forth, to the effect that no more slave States should be admitted. I agreed with you then, that if the President took such position he would violate the obligations of his office, and be faithless to the trust which you had reposed in him. I agreed with you then, that the exclusion of a State, because it was slaveholding, would be such an offence against your equality as would demand at your hands the vindication of your rights. What has been the result? The convention framed the constitution, submitted only the clause relating to slavery to a popular vote, and applied for admission. The President in his annual message referred in favorable terms to the application, then not formally made, and when the Constitution reached him transmitted it to Congress with a special message, in which he fully and emphatically maintained the right of admission.

After the convention had adjourned, Mr. Stanton, acting Governor of the Territory, called and extra session of the Freesoil Legislature, which has been elected, and it passed an act to submit the whole constitution to a popular vote. The President removed him from office,--a further evidence of the sincerity with which he was fulfilling your expectations in relation to Kansas. And it gives me pleasure here to say of him, what I am assured I can now say with confidence, that he will not shrink a hair's breadth from the position he has taken, but will move another step in advance, and fall, if fall he must, manfully upholding the rights and defying the insolence of ill-gotten power.

When the bill was presented to the Senate for the admission of the State of Kansas, after a long discussion, it was adopted, with a provision which required the State after admission to relinquish its claim to all the land asked for in its ordinance, except 5,000,000 acres, that being the largest amount which had been ever granted to a State at the period of its admission. There was also a provision declaratory of the right of the people to change their constitution at any time; though the instrument itself had restricted them for a term of years. I considered both those provisions objectionable; the first, because it was directory of legislation to be enacted by a State; and the second, because it was inviting to a disregard of the fundamental law, and had too much the seeming of a concession to the anti-slavery feeling which was impatient for a change of the constitution. That bill failed in the House, and was succeeded by a bill of the Opposition which recognized the right of Kansas to be admitted with a pro-slavery constitution, provided it should be adopted by a popular vote. This also failed, and in the division between the two Houses, a com- {sic}

As there has been much diversity of opinion in relation to that law, and I think much misapprehension as to its character, I will be pardoned for speaking of it somewhat minutely.

When it was known that the Conference Committee had prepared a bill, I mittee of conference was appointed, which framed the bill that became a law. being at the time confined to my house by disease, invited my colleague and the Representatives from the State to visit me, that we might confer together and decide upon the course which we would pursue. Before the evening of our meeting, a distinguished member of the House of Representatives, a member of the Committee, called and read to me the bill which they had prepared. It contained some features which I considered objectionable. He concurred with me, and promised to use his efforts to have them stricken out. When the Mississippi delegation assembled, our conference was full, and marked by the desire, first to protect the rights of our State, and secondly, to secure unanimity of action by its delegation. The objections which were urged, referred, as my memory serves me, entirely to the features which I had reason to hope would be stricken out. One of the delegation announced an unwillingness to support the proposed modification of the Senate proposition, lest it should be considered as yielding the point on which we had insisted that Congress could not require the Constitution to be submitted to a popular vote. I refer to the lamented Quitman, whose sincere devotion to Southern interests, no one, who knew him, could question. I regretted that he deemed it necessary to vote, finally, against the measure, but I honor the motive which governed his course.

The ordinance which was attached to the Constitution, was not a part of it, but a condition annexed to the application for admission. If Congress had stricken the ordinance out, the effect, I believe, would have been that of admitting the State without any reservation of the public land; would have transferred as an attribute of sovereignty the useful as well as the eminent domain. The Southern Senators who received the soubriquet of Southern ultras, held that position in 1850, in relation to the public lands of California, and it constituted one of their objections to the admission of that State at the time it was effected. To modify the ordinance, that is to change the condition on which the inhabitants of Kansas proposed to enter into the Union was necessarily to give them the right to withdraw their proposition.

It remained then for Congress if they reduced the amount of land asked for in the ordinance, either to provide the mode in which the inhabitants should accept or reject the modification or leave them to do it in such manner as they might adopt. The convention was defunct, the legislature was black republican and thought to be entitled to little confidence, and it seemed to be better that Congress should itself provide the mode of ascertaining the public will than leave that duty to the territorial legislature, such as it was believed and proven to be. It was a mere question of expediency, and I think the best course was pursued.

To have admitted the State without modification of the ordinance, would have been to grant five times as much of the public land as had ever been given to a State at the period of admission.

There was nothing to justify such a discrimination, and otherwise the State could not be admitted without referring the question or violating the principle of State sovereignty.

As a condition precedent, the general government may require the recognition of its right to control the primary disposal of the land, but can have no right to impose a condition with the mandate that it shall be subsequently fulfiled and no power to enforce the mandate if the State admitted should refuse to comply. Not for all the land in Kansas, not for all the land between the Missouri and the Pacific ocean, not for all the land of the continent of North America, would I agree that the federal government should have the power to coerce a State.

The necessity for having all conditions agreed upon before the admission of a State was demonstrated by Mr. Soule, in 1850, in the discussion of the bill for the admission of California. Mr. Webster replied to him but did not answer his argument, and the course of events seems likely to verify all that Senator Soule foretold.

Of the three methods which were supposable, I think Congress adopted the best; it was the only one which was attainable and secured all which was of value to the South. It was the admission by Congress of a State with a pro-slavery Constitution; it was the triumph of the principle that forbade Congress to interfere either as to the matter of the Constitution or the manner in which it should be formed and adopted.

The refusal of the inhabitants to accept the reduced endowment offered to them, and their decision to remain in a territorial condition, was, in my opinion, wise on their part and fortunate on ours. The late Governor, Denver, has forcibly pointed out to them their want of means to support a State government, and the propriety of giving their first attention to the establishment of order and the development of their internal resources. There were many reasons to doubt the fitness of the inhabitants of Kansas to be admitted as a State.

The condition of the country and the previous legislation of Congress made the case exceptional, and, in my judgment, justified the course adopted. I have, therefore, no apology or regret to offer in the case.

The Northern opponents of the measure have, among other denunciatory epithets, applied to it those of "bribery" and "coercion." "Bribery" to give less by twenty millions of acres of land than was claimed, and "coercion" to leave them to the option of receiving the usual endowment, or waiting until they had an amount of population which would give some assurance of their ability to maintain a State government. Though such is the requirement of the law, and designed to secure exemption from the mischievous agitation which has for several years disturbed the country and benefitted only the demagogues who make a trade of politics, we may scarcely hope to escape from a renewal of the agitation which has been found so profitable. The next phase of the question will probably be in the form of what is termed an "enabling act,"--a favorite measure with the advocates of "squatter sovereignty," who, claiming for the inhabitants of a Territory all the power of the people of a State, nevertheless consider it necessary that Congress should confer the power to form a Constitution and apply as a State. Congress has given authority for admission in some cases, but I think it better to avoid than to follow the precedent. Not that I am concerned for the doctrine of "squatter sovereignty," but that I would guard against the mischievous error of considering the federal government as the parent of States, and would restrict it to the function of admitting new States into the Union, barring all pretension to the power of creating them.

It seems now to be probable that the Abolitionists and their allies will have control of the next House of Representatives, and it may be well inferred from their past course that they will attempt legislation both injurious and offensive to the South. I have an abiding faith that any law which violates our constitutional rights, will be met with a veto by the present Executive.-- But should the next House of Representatives be such as would elect an Abolition President, we may expect that the election will be so conducted as probably to defeat a choice by the people and devolve the election upon the House.

Whether by the House or by the people, if an Abolitionist be chosen President of the United States, you will have presented to you the question of whether you will permit the government to pass into the hands of your avowed and implacable enemies. Without pausing for your answer, I will state my own position to be that such a result would be a species of revolution by which the purposes of the Government would be destroyed and the observance of its mere forms entitled to no respect.

In that event, in such manner as should be most expedient, I should deem it your duty to provide for your safety outside of a Union with those who have already shown the will, and would have acquired the power, to deprive you of your birthright and to reduce you to worse than the colonial dependence of your fathers.

The master mind of the so-called Republican party, Senator Seward, has in a. recent speech at Rochester, announced the purpose of his party to dislodge the Democracy from the possession of the federal Government, and assigns as a reason the friendship of that party for what he denominates the slave system. He declares the Union between the States having slave labor and free labor to be incompatible, and announces that one or the other must disappear. He even asserts that it was the purpose of the framers of the Government to destroy slave property, and cites as evidence of it, the provision for an amendment of the Constitution. He seeks to alarm his auditors by assuring them of the purpose on the part of the South and the Democratic party to force slavery upon all the States of the Union. Absurd as all this may seem to you, and incredulous as you may be of its acceptance by any intelligent portion of the citizens of the United States, I have reason to believe that it has been inculcated to no small extent in the Northern mind.

It requires but a cursory examination of the Constitution of the United States; but a partial knowledge of its history and of the motives of the men who formed it, to see how utterly fallacious it is to ascribe to them the purpose of interfering with the domestic institutions of any of the States. But if a disrespect for that instrument, a fanatical disregard of its purposes, should ever induce a majority, however large, to seek by amending the Constitution, to pervert it from its original object, and to deprive you of the equality which your fathers bequeathed to you, I say let the star of Mississippi be snatched from the constellation to shine by its inherent light, if it must be so, through all the storms and clouds of war.

The same dangerously powerful man describes the institution of slavery as degrading to labor, as intolerant and inhuman, and says the white laborer among us is not enslaved only because he cannot yet be reduced to bondage. Where he learned his lesson, I am at a loss to imagine; certainly not by observation, for you all know that by interest, if not by higher motive, slave labor bears to capital as kind a relation as can exist between them anywhere; that it removes from us all that controversy between the laborer and the capitalist, which has filled Europe with starving millions and made their poor houses an onerous charge. You too know, that among us, white men have an equality resulting from a presence of the lower caste, which cannot exist where white men fill the position here occupied by the servile race. The mechanic who comes among us, employing the less intellectual labor of the African, takes the position which only a master-workman occupies where all the mechanics are white, and therefore it is that our mechanics hold their position of absolute equality among us.

I say to you here as I have said to the Democracy of New York, if it should ever come to pass that the Constitution shall be perverted to the destruction of our rights so that we shall have the mere right as a feeble minority unprotected by the barrier of the Constitution to give an ineffectual negative vote in the Halls of Congress, we shall then bear to the federal government the relation our colonial fathers did to the British crown, and if we are worthy of our lineage we will in that event redeem our rights even if it be through the process of revolution. And it gratifies me to be enabled to say that no portion of the speech to which I have referred was received with more marked approbation by the Democracy there assembled than the sentiment which has just been cited. I am happy also to state that during the past summer I heard in many places, what previously I had only heard from the late President Pierce, the declaration that whenever a Northern army should be assembled to march for the subjugation of the South, they would have a battle to fight at home before they passed the limits of their own State, and one in which our friends claim that the victory will at least be doubtful.

Now, as in 1851, I hold separation from the Union by the State of Mississippi to be the last remedy--the final alternative. In the language of the venerated Calhoun I consider the disruption of the Union as a great though not the greatest calamity. I would cling tenaciously to our constitutional Government, seeing as I do in the fraternal Union of equal States the benefit to all and the fulfilment of that high destiny which our fathers hoped for and left it for their sons to attain. I love the flag of my country with even more than a filial affection. Mississippi gave me in my boyhood to her military service. For many of the best years of my life I have followed that flag and upheld it on fields where if I had fallen it might have been claimed as my winding sheet. When I have seen it surrounded by the flags of foreign countries, the pulsations of my heart have beat quicker with every breeze which displayed its honored stripes and brilliant constellation. I have looked with veneration on those stripes as recording the original size of our political family and with pride upon that constellation as marking the family's growth; I glory in the position which Mississippi's star holds in the group; but sooner than see its lustre dimmed--sooner than see it degraded from its present equality-would tear it from its place to be set even on the perilous ridge of battle as a sign round which

Mississippi's best and bravest should gather to the harvest-home of death.

As when I had the privilege of addressing the Legislature a year ago, so now do I urge you to the needful preparation to meet whatever contingency may befall us. The maintenance of our rights against a hostile power is a physical problem and cannot be solved by mere resolutions. Not doubtful of what the heart will prompt, it is not the less proper that due provision should be made for physical necessities. Why should not the State have an armory for the repair of arms, for the alteration of old models so as to make them conform to the improved weapons of the present day, and for the manufacture on a limited scale of new arms, including cannon and their carriages; the casting of shot and shells, and the preparation of fixed ammunition?

Such preparation will not precipitate us upon the trial of secession, for I hold now, as in 1850, that Mississippi's patriotism will hold her to the Union as long as it is constitutional, but it will give to our conduct the character of earnestness of which mere paper declarations have somewhat deprived us; it will strengthen the hands of our friends at the North, and in the event that separation shall be forced upon us, we shall be prepared to meet the contingency with whatever remote consequences may follow it, and give to manly hearts the happy assurance that manly arms will not fail to protect the gentle beauty which blesses our land and graces the present occasion.

You are already progressing in the construction of railroads which, whilst they facilitate travel, increase the products of the State and the reward of the husbandman, are a great element of strength by the means they afford for rapid combination at any point where it may be desirable to concentrate our forces. To those already in progress I hope one will soon be added to connect the interior of the State with the best harbor upon our

Gulf coast. When this shall be completed a trade will be opened to that point which will produce direct importation and exportation to the great advantage of the planter as well as all consumers of imported goods; and furnishing "exchange," will protect us from such revulsion as was suffered last fall when during a period of entire prosperity at home, our market was paralyzed by failures in New York.

The contemplated improvement in the levee system, will give to our people a mine of untold wealth; and as we progress in the development of our resources and the increase of our power, so will we advance in State pride and the ability to maintain principles far higher in value than mountains of gold or oceans of pearl.

But I find myself running into those visions which have hung before me from my boyhood up; which at home and abroad have been the hope constantly attending upon me, and which the cold wing of time has been unable to wither. I am about to leave you to discharge the duties of the high trust with which you have honored me. I go with the same love for Mississippi which has always animated me; with the same confidence in her people, which has cheered me in the darkest hour. As often as I may return to you, I feel secure of myself, and say I shall come back unchanged. Or should the Providence which has so often kindly protected me, not permit me to return again, my last prayer will be for the honor, the glory and the happiness of Mississippi.

www.ingramcontent.com/pod-product-compliance
Lightning Source LLC
Chambersburg PA
CBHW051549010526
44118CB00022B/2631